THE DIGNITY

AND

VOCATION

OF

WOMEN

Mulieris Dignitatem

Together! recognizes the generous contributions of the following who have made this publication possible:

Sister Mary Jeremiah, O.P., STD.

Genevieve Kineke

Paul and Libbie Sellors

THE DIGNITY
AND
VOCATION
OF
WOMEN

Study Guide

Together!

Mulieris Dignitatem text reprinted
from *L'Ossevatore Romano*

Together!

Together, Inc.
3205 Roosevelt Street NE • St Anthony MN 55418
www.togetherinc.net
ISBN 978-1-933463-10-0
ISBN 1-933463-10-4

THE DIGNITY AND VOCATION OF WOMEN

TABLE OF CONTENTS

ON THE DIGNITY AND VOCATION OF WOMEN

MULIERIS DIGNITATEM

Apostolic Letter of the Supreme Pontiff John Paul II
On the Occasion of the Marian Year

Venerable Brothers and dear Sons and Daughters, Health and the Apostolic Blessing.

SESSION ONE - Articles 1-3

I
INTRODUCTION

A Sign of the Times

1. The dignity and the vocation of women — a subject of constant human and Christian reflection — have gained exceptional prominence in recent years. This can be seen, for example, *in the statements of the Church's Magisterium* present in various documents *of the Second Vatican Council,* which declares in its Closing Message: "The hour is coming, in fact has come, when the vocation of women is being acknowledged in its fullness, the hour in which women acquire in the world an influence, an effect and a power never hitherto achieved. That is why, at this moment when the human race is undergoing so deep a transformation, women imbued with a spirit of the Gospel can do so much to aid humanity in not falling."[1] *This Message* sums up what had already been expressed in the Council's teaching, specifically in the Pastoral Constitution *Gaudium et Spes*[2] and in the Decree on the Apostolate of the Laity *Apostolicam Actuositatem.*[3]

Similar thinking had already been put forth in the period before the Council, as can be seen in a number of Pope *Pius XII*'s Discourses[4] and in the Encyclical *Pacem in Terris* of Pope *John XXIII.*[5] After the Second Vatican Council, my predecessor *Paul VI* showed the relevance of this "sign of the times," when he conferred the title "Doctor of the Church" upon Saint Teresa of Jesus and Saint Catherine of Siena,[6] and likewise when, at the request of the 1971 Assembly of the Synod of Bishops, he set up *a special Commission* for the study of contemporary problems concerning the *"effective promotion of the dignity and the responsibility of women."*[7] In one of his Discourses Paul VI said: "Within Christianity, more than in any other religion, and since its very beginning, women have had a special dignity, of which the New Testament shows us many important aspects...; it is evident that women are meant to form part of the living and working structure of Christianity in so prominent a manner that perhaps not all their potentialities have yet been made clear."[8]

The Fathers of the recent Assembly of the Synod of Bishops (October 1987), which was devoted to "The Vocation and Mission of the Laity in the Church and in the World Twenty Years after the Second Vatican Council," once more dealt with the dignity and vocation of women. One of their recommendations was for a further study of

1

the anthropological and theological bases that are needed in order to solve the problems connected with the meaning and dignity of being a woman and being a man. It is a question of understanding the reason for and the consequences of the Creator's decision that the human being should always and only exist as a woman or a man. It is only by beginning from these bases, which make it possible to understand the greatness of the dignity and vocation of women, that one is able to speak of their active presence in the Church and in society.

This is what I intend to deal with in this document. The Post-Synodal Exhortation, which will be published later, will present proposals of a pastoral nature on the place of women in the Church and in society. On this subject the Fathers offered some important reflections, after they had taken into consideration the testimonies of the lay Auditors — both women and men — from the particular Churches throughout the world.

The Marian Year

2. The last Synod took place *within the Marian Year*, which gives special thrust to the consideration of this theme, as the Encyclical *Redemptoris Mater* points out.[9] This Encyclical develops and updates the Second Vatican Council's teaching contained in Chapter VIII of the Dogmatic Constitution on the Church *Lumen Gentium*. The title of this chapter is significant: *"The Blessed Virgin Mary, the Mother of God, in the Mystery of Christ and of the Church."* Mary — the "woman" of the Bible (cf. *Gen* 3:15; *Jn.* 2:4; 19:16) — intimately belongs to the salvific mystery of Christ, and is therefore also present in a special way in the mystery of the Church. Since "the Church is in Christ as a sacrament. . . of intimate union with God and of the unity of the whole human race,"[10] the special presence of the Mother of God in the mystery of the Church makes us think *of the exceptional link between this "woman" and the whole human family*. It is a question here of every man and woman, all the sons and daughters of the human race, in whom from generation to generation a *fundamental inheritance* is realized, the inheritance that belongs to all humanity and that is linked with the mystery of the biblical "beginning": "God created man in his own image, in the image of God he created him; male and female he created them"(*Gen* 1:27).[11]

This eternal *truth about the human being*, man and woman — a truth which is immutably fixed in human experience — *at the same time constitutes the mystery which only in "the Incarnate Word takes on light...* (since) Christ fully reveals man to himself and makes his supreme calling clear," as the Council teaches.[12] In this "revealing of man to himself," do we not need to find a special place for that "woman" who was the Mother of Christ? Cannot the *"message" of Christ,* contained in the Gospel, which has as its background the whole of Scripture, both the Old and the New Testament, say much to the Church and to humanity about the dignity of women and their vocation?

This is precisely what is meant to be the common thread running throughout the present document, which fits into the broader context of the Marian Year, as we approach the end of the second millennium after Christ's birth and the beginning of the third. And it seems to me that the best thing is to *give this text the style and character of a meditation.*

II
WOMAN-MOTHER OF GOD
(*THEOTÓKOS*)

Union with God

3. "When the time had fully come, *God sent forth his son, born of woman."* With these words of his Letter to the Galatians (4:4), the Apostle Paul links together the principal moments which essentially determine the fulfillment of the mystery "pre-determined in God" (cf. *Eph* 1:9). The Son, the Word one in substance with the Father, becomes man, born of a woman, at "the fullness of time." This event leads *to the turning point* of man's history on earth, understood as salvation history. It is significant that Saint Paul does not call the Mother of Christ by her own name "Mary," but calls her "woman": this coincides with the words of the Proto-evangelium in the Book of Genesis (cf. 3:15). She is that "woman" who is present in the central salvific event which marks the "fullness of time": this event is realized in her and through her.

Thus there begins *the central event, the key event in the history of salvation:* the Lord's Paschal Mystery. Perhaps it would be worthwhile to reconsider it from the point of view of man's spiritual history, understood in the widest possible sense, and as this history is expressed through the different world religions. Let us recall at this point the words of the Second Vatican Council: *"People look to the various religions for answers* to those profound mysteries of the human condition which, today, even as in olden times, deeply stir the human heart: What is a human being? What is the meaning and purpose of our life? What is goodness and what is sin? What gives rise to our sorrows, and to what intent? Where lies the path to true happiness? What is the truth about death, judgment and retribution beyond the grave? What, finally, is *that ultimate and unutterable mystery which engulfs our being,* and from which we take our origin and towards which we move?"[13] "From ancient times down to the present, there has existed among different peoples a certain perception of that hidden power which is present in the course of things and in the events of human life; at times, indeed, recognition can be found of a Supreme Divinity or even a Supreme Father."[14]

Against the background of this broad panorama, which testifies to the aspirations of the human spirit in search of God — at times as it were "groping its way" (cf. *Acts* 17:27) — the "fullness of time" spoken of in Paul's Letter emphasizes *the response of God himself,* "in whom we live and move and have our being" (cf. *Acts* 17:28). This is the God who "in many and various ways spoke of old to our fathers by the prophets, but in these last days has spoken to us by a Son" (*Heb* 1:1-2). The sending of this Son, one in substance with the Father, as a man "born of woman," constitutes the culminating and *definitive point of God's self-revelation to humanity.* This self-revelation is salvific in character, as the Second Vatican Council teaches in another passage: "In his goodness and wisdom, God chose to reveal himself and to make known to us the hidden purpose of his will (cf. *Eph* 1:9) by which through Christ, the Word made flesh, man has access to the Father in the Holy Spirit and comes to share in the divine nature (cf. *Eph* 2:18; *2 Pt* 1:4)."[15]

3

A woman is to be found *at the center of this salvific event.* The self-revelation of God, who is the inscrutable unity of the Trinity, is outlined *in the Annunciation at Nazareth.* "Behold, you will conceive in your womb and bear a son, and you shall call his name Jesus. He will be great, and will be called the Son of the Most High" — "How shall this be, since I have no husband?" — "The Holy Spirit will come upon you, and the power of the Most High will overshadow you; therefore the child to be born will be called holy, the Son of God. . . . For with God nothing will be impossible" (cf. *Lk* 1:31-37).[16]

It may be easy to think of this event *in the setting* of the *history of Israel,* the Chosen People of which Mary is a daughter, but it is also easy to think of it in the context of all the different ways in which humanity has always sought to answer the fundamental and definitive questions which most beset it. Do we not find in the Annunciation at Nazareth the beginning of that definitive answer by which *God himself "attempts to calm people's hearts"?*[17] It is not just a matter here of God's words revealed through the Prophets; rather with this response "the Word is truly made flesh" (cf. *Jn.* 1:14). Hence *Mary* attains *a union with God that exceeds* all the expectations of the human spirit. It even exceeds the expectations of all Israel, in particular the daughters of this Chosen People, who, on the basis of the promise, could hope that one of their number would one day become the mother of the Messiah. Who among them, however, could have imagined that the promised Messiah would be "the Son of the Most High"? On the basis of the Old Testament's monotheistic faith such a thing was difficult to imagine. Only by the power of the Holy Spirit, who "overshadowed" her, was Mary able to accept what is "impossible with men, but not with God" (cf. *Mk* 10:27).

QUESTIONS - Session One

Our study of this Apostolic Letter, "On the Dignity and Vocation of Women," is divided under four major headings to illustrate woman's relationship to Jesus Christ.

Women and Jesus Christ -- Eternal Word of God

1. Pope John Paul II quotes from the closing message of the Second Vatican Council in his opening paragraph:
    > "The hour is coming, in fact has come, when the vocation of women is being acknowledged in its fullness, the hour in which women acquire in the world an influence, an effect and a power never hitherto achieved. That is why, at this moment when the human race is undergoing so deep a transformation, women imbued with a spirit of the Gospel can do so much to aid humanity in not falling."[1]

    Q. **Considering the state of the family, why is the Gospel message so important to mankind today?**

2. Q. **Identify some of the areas of confusion in the role of women in today's society.**

3. The Holy Father recognizes the many areas of confusion in society, and, in writing this document, wishes to accomplish three objectives:
    a. to show esteem for women,
    b. to consider the excellence of the feminine genius
    c. to address modern feminism.

    Q. **What were the original feminists trying to address? Were there inherent injustices in various cultures before the sexual revolution began in the West?**

---

[1] *Address of Pope Paul VI to Women* (December 8, 1965).

4. Q. Why is it important to look at what the Church is saying about the true dignity of women? What ethos or credibility does the Church have in this regard?

5. Q. Why does the Pope begin by speaking of Mary and the Marian Year?

See Supplement: *The Common Thread.*

6. Chapter 2 of *Mulieris Dignitatem* returns to themes discussed in *Redemptoris Mater*; God sent forth His Son born of a woman. The culmination and fullness of God's self-revelation is the Incarnation of the Eternal Word as a human being. God becomes what we are so that we might become what He is. God unites Himself with humanity through Mary's "Fiat," so we can share in the Divine Life of the Trinity.
Q. **In what ways can we respond to so great a gift?**

7. Continuing with the themes of *Redemptoris Mater*: The Eternal Word of the Father became man, born of a woman in the fullness of time. Mary is the *Theotokos*, a Greek term meaning God-bearer, meaning that she is indeed the Mother of God. Mary's new name, "Full of Grace," reveals both a supernatural reality and a vocation. She has a special role in the redemptive work of her Son. To serve is to reign.
Q. **How does the fullness of time reveal the extraordinary dignity of the Woman?**

The Common Thread

There is a common thread running through *Mulieris Dignitatem* and all that the Church did in preparing for this Third Millennium we now live in.

Throughout his pontificate, John Paul II repeated this truth: "Christ fully reveals man to himself and makes his supreme calling clear" (2; cf. *Gaudium et Spes* 22). Mary has a special place in this "revealing." She is a turning point in salvation history.

If Christ reveals what it means to be human, then we should listen and follow him. Women, after the example of Mary, have a special part to play in the Third Millennium. Each of the three years immediately leading up to the Millennium were dedicated to one of the Persons of the Trinity with Mary as our model:[2]

- devoted to Christ and the virtue of **faith**; to contemplate Mary in the mystery of her divine motherhood
- dedicated to the Holy Spirit and the virtue of **hope**; to imitate Mary as the woman who was docile to the Spirit
- focused on the Father and the virtue of **charity**; to consider Mary as the highly favored daughter of the Father and perfect model for believers

Take these to heart and be a true woman of the Third Millenium.

---

[2] Pope John Paul II, *As the Third Millennium Draws Near* (*Tertio Mellennio Adveniente*), November 10, 1994.

Theotókos

4. Thus the "fullness of time" manifests the extraordinary dignity of the "woman." On the one hand, this dignity consists *in the supernatural elevation to union with God* in Jesus Christ, which determines the ultimate finality of the existence of every person both on earth and in eternity. From this point of view, the "woman" is the representative and the archetype of the whole human race: she *represents the humanity* which belongs to all human beings, both men and women. On the other hand, however, the event at Nazareth highlights a form of union with the living God which can *only belong to the "woman,"* Mary: *the union between mother and son.* The Virgin of Nazareth truly becomes the Mother of God.

This truth, which Christian faith has accepted from the beginning, was solemnly defined at the Council of Ephesus (431 A.D.).[18] In opposition to the opinion of Nestorius, who held that Mary was only the mother of the man Jesus, this Council emphasized the essential meaning of the motherhood of the Virgin Mary. At the moment of the Annunciation, by responding with her *"fiat,"* Mary conceived a man who was the Son of God, of one substance with the Father. Therefore *she is truly the Mother of God, because motherhood concerns the whole person,* not just the body, nor even just human "nature." In this way the name *"Theotókos"* — Mother of God — became the name proper to the union with God granted to the Virgin Mary.

The particular union of the "Theotókos" with God — which fulfills in the most eminent manner the supernatural predestination to union with the Father which is granted to every human being *(filii in Filio)* — is a pure grace and, as such, *a gift of the Spirit.* At the same time, however, through her response of faith Mary exercises her free will and thus fully shares with her personal and feminine "I" in the event of the Incarnation. With her *"fiat," Mary becomes the authentic subject* of that union with God which was realized in the mystery of the Incarnation of the Word, who is of one substance with the Father. All of God's action in human history at all times respects the free will of the human "I". And such was the case with the Annunciation at Nazareth.

"To Serve Means to Reign"

5. This event is clearly *interpersonal in character:* it is a dialogue. We only understand it fully if we place the whole conversation between the Angel and Mary in the context of the words: "full of grace."[19] The whole Annunciation dialogue reveals the essential dimension of the event, namely, its *supernatural* dimension $(\varkappa\varepsilon\chi\alpha\rho\iota\tau\omega\mu\acute{\varepsilon}\nu\eta)$. Grace never casts nature aside or cancels it out, but rather perfects it and ennobles it. Therefore the *"fullness of grace"* that was granted to the Virgin of Nazareth, with a view to the fact that she would become *"Theotókos," also signifies the fullness of the perfection of"* what is characteristic of woman," of *"what is feminine."* Here we find ourselves, in a sense, at the culminating point, the archetype, of the personal dignity of women.

When Mary responds to the words of the

9

heavenly messenger with her "fiat," she who is "full of grace" feels the need to express her personal relationship to the gift that has been revealed to her, saying: *"Behold, I am the handmaid of the Lord"* (*Lk* 1:38). This statement should not be deprived of its profound meaning, nor should it be diminished by artificially removing it from the overall context of the event and from the full content of the truth revealed about God and man. In the expression "handmaid of the Lord," one senses Mary's complete awareness of being a creature of God. The word "handmaid," near the end of the Annunciation dialogue, is inscribed throughout the whole history of the Mother and the Son. In fact, this *Son,* who is the true and consubstantial "Son of the Most High," will often say of himself, especially at the culminating moment of his mission: "The Son of Man came not to be served but to serve" (*Mk* 10:45).

At all times Christ is aware of being "the servant of the Lord" according to the prophecy of Isaiah (cf. *Is* 42:1; 49:3, 6; 52:13) which includes the essential content of his messianic mission, namely, his awareness of being the Redeemer of the world. From the first moment of her divine motherhood, of her union with the Son whom "the Father sent into the world, that the world might be saved through him" (cf. *Jn.* 3:17), *Mary takes her place within Christ's messianic service.*[20] It is precisely this service which constitutes the very foundation of that Kingdom in which "to serve. . . means to reign."[21] Christ, the "Servant of the Lord," will show all people the royal dignity of service, the dignity which is joined in the closest possible way to the vocation of every person.

Thus, by considering the reality "Woman — Mother of God," we enter in a very appropriate way into this Marian Year meditation. *This reality also determines the essential horizon of reflection on the dignity and the vocation of women.* In anything we think, say or do concerning the dignity and the vocation of women, our thoughts, hearts and actions must not become detached from this horizon. The dignity of every human being and the vocation corresponding to that dignity find their definitive measure in *union with God.* Mary, the woman of the Bible, is the most complete expression of this dignity and vocation. For no human being, male or female, created in the image and likeness of God, can *in any* way attain fulfillment apart from this image and likeness.

QUESTIONS - Session Two

1. In Session 1, we learned that the "fullness of time manifests the extraordinary dignity of the woman." Christ becoming man through a woman imparts great dignity — on both women and all of humanity, whose likeness He assumed in the flesh. *The dignity of women is both a fact and a vocation.* It is a fact imparted by Christ's Incarnation; and giving birth to Christ is the perfection of what is feminine, placing motherhood at the foundation of the woman's vocation. It is an active characteristic, indicating the call to receive, develop and giving birth to Christ in the hearts of people.

    The fullness of feminine holiness is modeled by Mary, who — being "full of grace" — is the person most united to God. As a woman, this high dignity reflects upon all other women who follow her example. *The dignity and vocation of each woman are found in union with God.*

    Q. How can you be a spiritual mother, giving birth to Christ in the hearts of the people in your daily life?

2. There is another characteristic or special quality of women pointed out by the Holy Father. It is expressed by Mary's response, "I am the handmaid of the Lord."

    Q. Why is "handmaiden" such a charged word that alienates many women?

3. **Q. How does Mary's understanding of her vocation model humility to all her children in the faith?**

4. Q. How does the Christian vision of service differ from the world's view?

5. Q. How do you view service? Is it hard or easy? Enriching or impoverishing?

6. Q. How should the authentically feminine response differ from the feminist reaction that has been widely manifest in the last 40 years?

III
THE IMAGE AND LIKENESS OF GOD

The Book of Genesis

6. Let us enter into the setting of the biblical "beginning." In it the revealed truth concerning man as "the image and likeness" of God constitutes the immutable *basis of all Christian anthropology.*[22] "God created man in his own image, in the image of God he created him; male and female he created them" (*Gen* 1:27). This concise passage contains the fundamental anthropological truths: man is the highpoint of the whole order of creation in the visible world; the human race, which takes its origin from the calling into existence of man and woman, crowns the whole work of creation; *both man and woman are human beings to an equal degree,* both are created *in God's image.* This image and likeness of God, which is essential for the human being, is passed on by the man and woman, as spouses and parents, to their descendants: "Be fruitful and multiply, and fill the earth and subdue it" (*Gen* 1:28). The Creator entrusts dominion over the earth to the human race, to all persons, to all men and women, who derive their dignity and vocation from the common "beginning."

In the Book of Genesis we find another description of the creation of man — man and woman (cf. 2:18-25) — to which we shall refer shortly. At this point, however, we can say that the biblical account puts forth the truth about the personal character of the human being. *Man is a person, man and woman equally so,* since both were created in the image and likeness of the personal God. What makes man like God is the fact that — unlike the whole world of other living creatures, including those endowed with senses *(animalia)* — man is also a rational being *(animal rationale).*[23] Thanks to this property, man and woman are able to "dominate" the other creatures of the visible world (cf. *Gen* 1:28).

The second description of the creation of man (cf. *Gen* 2:18-25) makes use of different language to express the truth about the creation of man, and especially of woman. In a sense the language is less precise, and, one might say, more descriptive and metaphorical, closer to the language of the myths known at the time. Nevertheless, we find no essential contradiction between the two texts. The text of *Gen* 2:18-25 helps us to understand better what we find in the concise passage of *Gen* 1:27-28. At the same time, if it is read together with the latter, it *helps us to understand even more profoundly* the fundamental *truth* which it contains *concerning man* created as man and woman in the image and likeness of God.

In the description found in *Gen* 2:18-25, the woman is created by God "from the rib" of the man and is placed at his side as another "I", as the companion of the man, who is alone in the surrounding world of living creatures and who finds in none of them a "helper" suitable for himself. Called into existence in this way, the woman is immediately recognized by the man as "flesh of his flesh and bone of his bones" (cf. *Gen* 2:23) and for this very reason she is called "woman." In biblical language this name indicates her essential identity with regard to man - 'is-'issah — something which unfortunately modern languages in general are unable to express:

13

"She shall be called woman ('issah) because she was taken out of man ('is)": *Gen* 2:23.

The biblical text provides sufficient bases for recognizing the essential equality of man and woman from the point of view of their humanity.[24] From the very beginning, both are persons, unlike the other living beings in the world about them. *The woman is another "I" in a common humanity.* From the very beginning they appear as a "unity of the two," and this signifies that the original solitude is overcome, the solitude in which man does not find "a helper fit for him" (*Gen* 2:20). Is it only a question here of a "helper" in activity, in "subduing the earth" (cf. *Gen* 1:28)? Certainly it is a matter of a life's companion, with whom, as a wife, the man can unite himself, becoming with her "one flesh" and for this reason leaving "his father and his mother" (cf. *Gen* 2:24). Thus in the same context as the creation of man and woman, the biblical account speaks of God's *instituting marriage* as an indispensable condition for the transmission of life to new generations, the transmission of life to which marriage and conjugal love are by their nature ordered: "Be fruitful and multiply, and fill the earth and subdue it" (*Gen* 1:28).

Person – Communion – Gift

7. By reflecting on the whole account found in *Gen* 2:18-25, and by interpreting it in light of the truth about the image and likeness of God (cf. *Gen* 1:26-27), we can *understand* even *more fully what constitutes the personal character* of the human being, thanks to which both man and woman are like God. For every individual is made in the image of God, insofar as he or she is a rational and free creature capable of

knowing God and loving him. Moreover, we read that man cannot exist "alone" (cf. *Gen* 2:18); he can exist only as a "unity of the two," and therefore *in relation to another human person.* It is a question here of a mutual relationship: man to woman and woman to man. Being a person in the image and likeness of God thus also involves existing in a relationship, in relation to the other "I". This is a prelude to the definitive self-revelation of the Triune God: a living unity in the communion of the Father, Son and Holy Spirit.

At the beginning of the Bible this is not yet stated directly. The whole Old Testament is mainly concerned with revealing the truth about the oneness and unity of God. Within this fundamental truth about God the New Testament will reveal the inscrutable mystery of God's inner life. *God,* who allows himself to be known by human beings through Christ, is the *unity of the Trinity:* unity in communion. In this way new light is also thrown on man's image and likeness to God, spoken of in the Book of Genesis. The fact that man "created as man and woman" is the image of God means not only that each of them individually is like God, as a rational and free being. It also means that man and woman, created as a "unity of the two" in their common humanity, are called to live in a communion of love, and in this way to mirror in the world the communion of love that is in God, through which the Three Persons love each other in the intimate mystery of the one divine life. The Father, Son and Holy Spirit, one God through the unity of the divinity, exist as persons through the inscrutable divine relationship. Only in this way can we understand the truth that God in himself is love (cf. *1 Jn.* 4:16).

The image and likeness of God in man, created as man and woman (in the analogy that can be presumed between Creator and creature), thus also expresses the "unity of the two" in a common humanity. This "unity of the two," which is a sign of interpersonal communion, *shows that the creation of man* is also marked by a certain likeness to the divine communion *("communio")*. This likeness is a quality of the personal being of both man and woman, and is also a call and a task. The foundation of the whole *human "ethos"* is rooted in the image and likeness of God which the human being bears within himself from the beginning. Both the Old and New Testament will develop that "ethos," which reaches its apex in the *commandment of love.*[25]

In the "unity of the two," man and woman are called from the beginning not only to exist "side by side" or "together," but they are also called *to exist mutually "one for the other."*

This also explains the meaning of the "help" spoken of in *Genesis* 2:18-25: "I will make him *a helper fit for him."* The biblical context enables us to understand this in the sense that the woman must "help" the man — and in his turn he must help her — first of all by the very fact of their "being human persons." In a certain sense this enables man and woman to discover their humanity ever anew and to confirm its whole meaning. We can easily understand that — on this fundamental level — it is a question of *a "help" on the part of both, and at the same time a mutual "help."* To be human means to be called to interpersonal communion. The text of *Genesis* 2:18-25 shows that marriage is the first and, in a sense, the fundamental dimension of this call. But it is not the only one. The whole of human history unfolds within the context of this call. In this history, on the basis of the principle of mutually being "for" the other, in interpersonal "communion," there develops in humanity itself, in accordance with God's will, the integration of *what is "masculine" and what is "feminine."* The biblical texts, from Genesis onwards, constantly enable us to discover the ground in which the truth about man is rooted, the solid and inviolable ground amid the many changes of human existence.

This truth also has to do with *the history of salvation.* In this regard a statement of the Second Vatican Council is especially significant. In the chapter on "The Community of Mankind" in the Pastoral Constitution *Gaudium et Spes,* we read: "The Lord Jesus, when he prayed to the Father 'that all may be one. . . as we are one' (*Jn.* 17:21-22), opened up vistas closed to human reason. For he implied a *certain likeness* between the union of the divine Persons and the union of God's children in truth and charity. This likeness reveals that man, who is the only creature on earth which God willed for its own sake, cannot fully find himself except through a sincere gift of self."[26]

With these words, the Council text presents a summary of the whole truth about man and woman — a truth which is already outlined in the first chapters of the Book of Genesis, and which is the structural basis of biblical and Christian anthropology. Man — whether man or woman — *is the only being among the creatures* of the visible world *that God the Creator "has willed for its own sake";* that creature is thus a person. Being a person means striving towards self-realization (the Council text speaks of self-discovery), which can only be achieved *"through a sincere gift of self."* The model for this interpretation of the person is God himself as Trinity, as a communion of Persons. To say that man is created in the image and likeness of God means that man is called to exist "for" others, to become a gift.

This applies to every human being, whether woman or man, who live it out in accordance with the special qualities proper to each. Within the framework of the present meditation on the dignity and vocation of women, this truth about being human constitutes the *indispensable point of departure.* Already in the Book of Genesis we can discern, in preliminary outline, the spousal character of the relationship between persons, which will serve as the basis for the subsequent development of the truth about motherhood, and about virginity, as two particular dimensions of the vocation of women in the light of divine Revelation. These two dimensions will find their loftiest expression at the "fullness of time" (cf. *Gal* 4:4) in the "woman" of Nazareth: the Virgin-Mother.

The anthropomorphism of biblical language

8. The presentation of man as "the image and likeness of God" at the very beginning of Sacred Scripture has *another significance too.* It is the key for understanding biblical Revelation as God's word about himself. Speaking about himself, whether through the prophets, or through the Son" (cf. *Heb* 1:1,2) who became man, *God speaks in human language,* using human concepts and images. If this manner of expressing himself is characterized by a certain anthropomorphism, the reason is that man

is "like" God: created in his image and likeness. But then, *God too* is in some measure "like man," and precisely because of this likeness, he can be humanly known. At the same time, the language of the Bible is sufficiently precise to indicate the limits of the "likeness," the limits of the "analogy." For biblical Revelation says that, while man's "likeness" to God is true, the *"non-likeness"*[27] which separates the whole of creation from the Creator is *still more essentially true.* Although man is created in God's likeness, God does not cease to be for him the one "who dwells in unapproachable light" (*1 Tim* 6:16): he is the "Different One," by essence the "totally Other."

This observation on the limits of the analogy — the limits of man's likeness to God in biblical language — must also be kept in mind when, in different passages of Sacred Scripture (especially in the Old Testament), we find *comparisons that attribute to God "masculine" or "feminine" qualities.* We find in these passages an indirect confirmation of the truth that both man and woman were created in the image and likeness of God. If there is a likeness between Creator and creatures, it is understandable that the Bible would refer to God using expressions that attribute to him both "masculine" and "feminine" qualities.

We may quote here some characteristic passages from the prophet Isaiah: "But Zion said, 'The Lord has forsaken me, my Lord has forgotten me.' *'Can a woman forget* her sucking child, that she should have no compassion on the son of her womb? Even these may forget, yet *I* will *not* forget you'" (49:14-15). And elsewhere: "*As* one whom his *mother* comforts, so will I comfort you; you shall be comforted in Jerusalem" (66:13). In the Psalms too God is compared to a caring mother: "Like a child quieted at its mother's breast; like a child that is quieted is my soul. O Israel, hope in the Lord" (*Ps* 131:2-3). In various passages the love of God who cares for his people is shown to be like that of a mother: thus, *like a mother God* "has carried" humanity, and in particular, his Chosen People, within his own womb; he has given birth to it in travail, has nourished and comforted it (cf. *Is* 42:14; 46:3-4). In many passages God's love is presented as the "masculine" love of the bridegroom and father (cf. *Hosea* 11:1-4; *Jer* 3:4-19), but also sometimes as the "feminine" love of a mother.

This characteristic of biblical language — its anthropomorphic way of speaking about God — *points* indirectly *to the mystery of the eternal "generating"* which belongs to the inner life of God. Nevertheless, in itself this "generating" has neither "masculine" nor "feminine" qualities. It is by nature totally divine. It is spiritual in the most perfect way, since "God is spirit" (*Jn.* 4:24) and possesses no property typical of the body, neither "feminine" nor "masculine." Thus even *"fatherhood" in God is completely divine* and free of the "masculine" bodily characteristics proper to human fatherhood. In this sense the Old Testament spoke of God as a Father and turned to him as a Father. Jesus Christ — who called God "Abba Father" (*Mk* 14:36), and who as the only-begotten and consubstantial Son placed this truth at the very center of his Gospel, thus establishing the norm of Christian prayer — referred to fatherhood in this ultra-corporeal, superhuman and completely divine sense. He spoke as the Son, joined to the Father by the eternal mystery of divine generation, and he did so while being at the same time the truly human Son of his Virgin Mother.

Although it is not possible to attribute human qualities to the eternal generation of the Word of God, and although the divine fatherhood does not possess "masculine" characteristics in a physical sense, we must nevertheless seek in God the absolute *model* of all *"generation"* among human beings. This would seem to be the sense of the Letter to the Ephesians: "I bow my knees before the Father, from whom every family in heaven and on earth is named" (3:14-15). All "generating" among creatures finds its primary model in that generating which in God is completely divine, that is, spiritual. All "generating" in the created world is to be likened to this absolute and uncreated model. Thus every element of human generation which is proper to man, and every element which is proper to woman, namely human *"fatherhood"* and *"motherhood,"* bears within itself a likeness to, or analogy with the divine "generating" and with that "fatherhood" which in God is "totally different," that is, completely spiritual and divine in essence; whereas in the human order, generation is proper to the "unity of the two": both are "parents," the man and the woman alike.

QUESTIONS - Session Three

1. Q. What is the basic Christian anthropology?[3] And in what ways are humans in the "image and likeness" of God?

   (See Supplement: *Equality, Creation & Marriage*)

2. Q. The second creation story gives further insights into our understanding of the human person. Discuss some of those insights.

3. Man was alone until the creation of woman. Because the Trinity is three Persons in one God, human beings living in a mutual self-giving relationship reflect the "image and likeness" of the triune God.
   - The man and woman are called to live in a communion of love. The great commandment of Jesus is, "Love one another" (*Jn* 13). Scripture also says, "God is love" (*1 Jn* 4:16).
   - The man and woman, as individuals, image God as free, rational beings. But also man and woman together, as a unity, image God in the communion of love.

   Q. Discuss specific ways that sacramental marriage draws on the Trinity as a guide for life-giving love.

4. Q. Even outside of marriage, consider how giving yourself to another enabled you to be more of a person: helped you grow in self-realization and self-discovery?

---

[3] Anthropology, from two Greek words meaning Man, human, and Study of. The English word means the study of humanity; the way to understand the human person.

5. The principle of analogy is a very important theological concept. It is the comparison of two things that are similar, yet different. This principle, used in Scripture, helps us speak of God Who is totally beyond us and of Whom we can really know very little. The similarities help our limited minds to grasp infinite ideas, and yet the limits of the analogies must always be kept in mind so that we don't limit the truths of God.

   Q. In speaking of biblical anthropomorphism,[4] the Pope refers to the principle of analogy. Using examples from Scripture, in what ways is God analogous to a father and in what ways is God analogous to a mother?

6. The most important attribute of God after that of His very essence (being "love") is that love is generative by nature.

   Q. How does "eternal generation," which belongs to the inner life of God differ from the masculine and feminine ways of generating life?

7. Q. Why do you think that God would ask us to consider him "Father" when by nature He is not masculine? What happens when we call God "Mother?"

---

[4] Anthropomorphism comes from two Greek words meaning, "man, human" and "form, shape". It means describing God with human characteristics. For example, God became angry; God hid his face.

Equality, Creation & Marriage

The Holy Father begins early in this document with an answer to the question of equality. It is important to clarify what we mean by "equality" even though we know that women are equal. Feminism, politically speaking, requires that "equal" means "same". Some of the results are:

- abortion - women can be sexually irresponsible, as some men have become
- freedom from child care
- combative military roles for women
- women in roles such as hockey (with men), cursing, etc., etc..
- women's liberation is in practice, often simply being as crude as some men.

Other extremes are Christian women who think that women are inferior creatures; or men who do not regard women as capable and intelligent. The Church offers a beautiful, balanced view to both of these sides. We find the answer in Genesis 1:27, "*God created man in his own image; in the image of God he created him; male and female he created them.*" Man refers to them, male and female (not the species male and the species female but the persons). The image of God is man – male & female *together*.

We know that the Incarnation beautifully illustrates and develops the fact that each individual human person is important to God. Each human person is created in His image. However, the Holy Father is saying more than this. He is saying that the male *with* the female reflects God's image more so than an individual reflects God's image (though that is also true). The male and female together are a communion of persons. Looking at the document we can see how the Pope develops this point.

Chapter 1 of this document speaks of "in the image of God He created them" and "in the command to "be fruitful and multiply," God entrusts dominion of earth to them. They then transmit this dignity to their descendants. Man is rational in the *collective* sense of male and female. This is God's likeness in them: *together* they have dominion over the earthly world (6).

The second creation account is different, but the Holy Father explains they are not contradictory, rather they help us to understand the creation story more deeply.

Woman is created from Adam's rib. The Holy Father quotes Hebrew, 'is – issah' showing how they are of one substance. "She shall be called woman ('issah'), because she is taken out of man ('is')." Adam and Adam – ness. (The idea is unclear in modern languages.)

To understand this, look at Adam's reaction to Eve. Adam does not say, "Good, now I can get some help around here." or "Get busy." or "What a doll!" Adam said, "Here at last is flesh of my flesh." *Adam recognizes himself.* Eve is a helper, but she is more than a helper, she is co-equal and co-founder of our human race. She is another "I" to Adam. From the beginning Adam and Eve are a "unity of two."

So remarkable is the unity of Adam and Eve, that here marriage is instituted — "for this reason a man leaves his father and mother and cleaves to his wife". They become one in love. You can see how this shows God's likeness. God exists as a unity — but at the same time — as Trinity; Father, Son, and Holy Spirit in perfect communion with each other in love. God is love. Man is to reflect that loving community, that mutual relationship of the Trinity.

Man's communion is to be in likeness of God and is expressed in the commandment to love God, and to love neighbor as yourself. The intention is that spouses are not just to work side by side, but to exist mutually, "one for the other." Help is not subordination but clearly assistance. It is mutual, male helping female and female helping male.

For further enrichment:
Read the June 25, 1995, *Letter to Women* Articles 7 & 8, Pope John Paul II.

Women and Jesus Christ - Redeemer

The "Beginning" and the Sin

9. "Although he was made by God in a state of justice, from the very dawn of history man abused his liberty, at the urging of the Evil One. Man set himself against God and sought to find fulfillment apart from God."[28] With these words the teaching of the last Council recalls the revealed doctrine about sin and in particular about that first sin, which is the "original" one. The biblical "beginning" — the creation of the world and of man in the world — *contains* in itself *the truth* about *this sin,* which can also be called the sin of man's "beginning" on the earth. Even though what is written in the Book of Genesis is expressed in the form of a symbolic narrative, as is the case in the description of the creation of man as male and female (cf. *Gen* 2:18-25), at the same time it reveals what should be called "the mystery of sin," and even more fully, "the mystery of evil" which exists in the world created by God.

It is not possible to read "the mystery of sin" without making reference to the whole truth about the "image and likeness" to God, which is the basis of biblical anthropology. This truth presents the creation of man as a special gift from the Creator, containing not only the foundation and source of the essential dignity of the human being — man and woman — in the created world, but also *the beginning of the call to both of them to share in the intimate life of God himself.* In the light of Revelation, *creation likewise means the beginning of salvation history.* It is precisely in this beginning that sin is situated and manifests itself as opposition and negation.

It can be said, paradoxically, that the sin presented in the third chapter of Genesis confirms the truth about the image and likeness of God in man, since this truth means freedom, that is, man's use of free will by choosing good or his abuse of it by choosing evil, against the will of God. In its essence, however, sin is a negation of God as Creator in his relationship to man, and of what God wills for man, from the beginning and for ever. Creating man and woman in his own image and likeness, God wills for them the fullness of good, or supernatural happiness, which flows from sharing in his own life. *By committing sin man rejects this gift* and at the same time wills to become "as God, knowing good and evil" (*Gen* 3:5), that is to say, deciding what is good and what is evil independently of God, his Creator. The sin of the first parents has its own human "measure": an interior standard of its own in man's free will, and it also has within itself a certain "diabolic" characteristic,[29] which is clearly shown in the Book of Genesis (3:15). Sin brings about a break in the original unity which man enjoyed in the state of original justice: union with God as the source of the unity within his own "I", in the mutual relationship between man and woman (*"communio personarum"*) as well as in regard to the external world, to nature.

The biblical description of original sin in the third chapter of Genesis in a certain way "distinguishes the roles" which the woman and the man had in it. This is also referred to later in certain passages of the

Bible, for example, Paul's Letter to Timothy: "For Adam was formed first, then Eve; and Adam was not deceived, but the woman was deceived and became a transgressor" (*1 Tim* 2:13-14). But there is no doubt that, independent of this "distinction of roles" in the biblical description, *that first sin is the sin of man,* created by God as male and female. It is also *the sin of the "first parents,"* to which is connected its hereditary character. In this sense we call it "original sin."

This sin, as already said, *cannot be properly understood without reference to the mystery of the creation* of the human being — man and woman — *in the image and likeness of God.* By means of this reference one can also understand the mystery of that "non-likeness" to God in which sin consists, and which manifests itself in the evil present in the history of the world. Similarly one can understand the mystery of that "non-likeness" to God, who "alone is good" (cf. *Mt* 19:17) and-the fullness of good. If sin's "non-likeness" to God, who is Holiness itself, presupposes "likeness" in the sphere of freedom and free will, it can then be said that for this very reason *the "non-likeness" contained in sin* is all the more tragic and sad. It must be admitted that God, as Creator and Father, is here wounded, "offended" — obviously offended — in the very heart of that gift which belongs to God's eternal plan for man.

At the same time, however, as the author of the evil of sin, *the human being — man and woman — is affected by it.* The third chapter of Genesis shows this with the words which clearly describe the new situation of man in the created world. It shows the perspective of "toil," by which man will earn his living (cf. *Gen* 3:17-19) and likewise the great "pain" with which the woman will give birth to her children (cf. Gen 3 :16). And all this is marked by the necessity of death, which is the end of human life on earth. In this way man, as dust, will "return to the ground, for out of it he was taken": "you are dust, and to dust you shall return" (cf. *Gen* 3:19).

These words are confirmed generation after generation. They do not mean that *the image and the likeness of God in the human being,* whether woman or man, has been destroyed by sin; they mean rather that it has been *"obscured"*[30] and in a sense *"diminished."* Sin in fact "diminishes" man, as the Second Vatican Council also recalls.[31] If man is the image and likeness of God by his very nature as a person, then his greatness and his dignity are achieved in the covenant with God, in union with him, in striving towards that fundamental unity which belongs to the internal "logic" of the very mystery of creation. This unity corresponds to the profound truth concerning all intelligent creatures and in particular concerning man, who among all the creatures of the visible world was elevated from the beginning through the eternal choice of God in Jesus: "He chose us in (Christ) before the foundation of the world, . . . He destined us in love to be his sons through Jesus Christ, according to the purpose of his will" (*Eph* 1:4-6). The biblical teaching taken as a whole enables us to say that predestination concerns all human persons, men and women, each and every one without exception.

"He shall rule over you"

10. The biblical description in the Book of Genesis outlines the truth about the consequences of man's sin, as it is shown by *the disturbance* of that original

relationship between man and woman which corresponds to their individual dignity as persons. A human being, whether male or female, is a person, and therefore, "the only creature on earth which God willed for its own sake"; and at the same time this unique and unrepeatable creature "cannot fully find himself except through a sincere gift of self."[32] Here begins the relationship of "communion" in which the "unity of the two" and the personal dignity of both man and woman find expression. Therefore when we read in the biblical description the words addressed to the woman: *"Your desire shall be for your husband, and he shall rule over you"* (*Gen* 3:16), we discover a break and a constant threat precisely in regard to this "unity of the two" which corresponds to the dignity of the image and likeness of God in both of them. But this threat is more serious for the woman, since domination takes the place of "being a sincere gift" and therefore living "for" the other: "he shall rule over you." This "domination" indicates the disturbance and *loss of the stability* of that *fundamental equality* which the man and the woman possess in the "unity of the two": and this is especially to the disadvantage of the woman, whereas only the equality resulting from their dignity as persons can give to their mutual relationship the character of an authentic *"communio personarum."* While the violation of this equality, which is both a gift and a right deriving from God the Creator, involves an element to the disadvantage of the woman, at the same time it also diminishes the true dignity of the man. Here we touch upon *an extremely sensitive point in the dimension of that "ethos"* which was originally inscribed by the Creator in the very creation of both of them in his own image and likeness.

This statement in Genesis 3:16 is of great significance. It implies a reference to the mutual relationship of man and woman *in marriage.* It refers to the desire born in the atmosphere of spousal love whereby the woman's "sincere gift of self" is responded to and matched by a corresponding "gift" on the part of the husband. Only on the basis of this principle can both of them, and in particular the woman, "discover themselves" as a true "unity of the two" according to the dignity of the person. The matrimonial union requires respect for and a perfecting of the true personal subjectivity of both of them. *The woman cannot become the "object" of "domination" and male "possession."* But the words of the biblical text directly concern original sin and its lasting consequences in man and woman. Burdened by hereditary sinfulness, they bear within themselves the constant *"inclination to sin,"* the tendency to go against the moral order which corresponds to the rational nature and dignity of man and woman as persons. This tendency is expressed in *a threefold concupiscence,* which Saint John defines as the lust of the eyes, the lust of the flesh and the pride of life (cf. *1 Jn.* 2:16). The words of the Book of Genesis quoted previously (3:16) show how this threefold concupiscence, the "inclination to sin," will burden the mutual relationship of man and woman.

These words of Genesis refer directly to marriage, but indirectly *they concern the different spheres of social life:* the situations in which the woman remains disadvantaged or discriminated against by the fact of being a woman. The revealed truth concerning the creation of the human being as male and female constitutes the principal argument against all the objectively injurious and unjust situations which contain and express the inheritance of the sin which all human beings bear within themselves. The books of Sacred Scripture confirm in various places *the actual existence of such situations* and at the same time proclaim the need for conversion, that is to say, for purification from evil and liberation from sin: from what offends neighbor, what "diminishes" man, not only the one who is offended but also the one who causes the offence. This is the unchangeable message of the Word revealed by God. In it is expressed the biblical "ethos" until the end of time.[33]

In our times the question of "women's rights" has taken on new significance in the broad context of the rights of the human person. *The biblical and evangelical message* sheds light on this cause, which is the object of much attention today, *by safeguarding the truth about the "unity" of the "two,"* that is to say the truth about that dignity and vocation that result from the specific diversity and personal originality of man and woman. Consequently, even the rightful opposition of women to what is expressed in the biblical words "He shall rule over you" (*Gen* 3:16) must not under any condition lead to the "masculinization" of women. In the name of liberation from male "domination," women must not appropriate to themselves male characteristics contrary to their own feminine "originality." There is a well-founded fear that if they take this path, women will not "reach fulfillment," but instead will *deform and lose what constitutes their essential richness.* It is indeed an enormous richness. In the biblical description, the words of the first man at the sight of the woman who had been created are words of admiration and enchantment, words which fill the whole history of man on earth.

The personal resources of femininity are certainly no less than the resources of masculinity: they are merely different. Hence a woman, as well as a man, must understand her "fulfillment" as a person, her dignity and vocation, on the basis of these resources, according to the richness of the femininity which she received on the day of creation and which she inherits as an expression of the "image and likeness of God" that is specifically hers. *The inheritance of sin* suggested by the words of the Bible — "Your desire shall be for your husband, and he shall rule over you" — *can be conquered* only by following this path. The overcoming of this evil inheritance is, generation after generation, the task of every human being, whether woman or man. For whenever man is responsible for offending a woman's personal dignity and vocation, he acts contrary to his own personal dignity and his own vocation.

Proto-evangelium

11. The Book of Genesis attests to the fact that sin is the evil at man's "beginning" and that since then its consequences weigh upon the whole human race. At the same time it contains *the first foretelling of victory* over evil, *over sin.* This is proved by the words which we read in Genesis 3:15, usually called the *"Proto-evangelium":* "I will put enmity between you and the woman, and between your seed and her seed; he shall bruise your head, and you shall bruise his heel." It is significant that the foretelling of the Redeemer contained in these words refers to "the woman." She is assigned the first place in the Proto-evangelium as the progenitrix of him who will be the Redeemer of man.[34] And since the redemption is to be accomplished through

26

a struggle against evil — through the "enmity" between the offspring of the woman and the offspring of him who, as "the father of lies" (*Jn.* 8:44), is the first author of sin in human history — it is also *an enmity between him and the woman.*

These words give us a comprehensive view of the whole of Revelation, first as a preparation for the Gospel and later as the Gospel itself. From this vantage point the two female figures, Eve and Mary, are joined under the *name of woman.*

The words of the Proto-evangelium, re-read in the light of the New Testament, express well the mission of woman in the Redeemer's salvific struggle against the author of evil in human history.

The comparison Eve-Mary constantly recurs in the course of reflection on the deposit of faith received from divine Revelation. It is one of the themes frequently taken up by the Fathers, ecclesiastical writers and theologians.[35] As a rule, from this comparison there emerges at first sight a difference, a contrast. *Eve,* as "the mother of all the living" (*Gen* 3:20), is *the witness to the biblical "beginning,"* which contains the truth about the creation of man made in the image and likeness of God and the truth about original sin. *Mary is the witness to the new "beginning"* and the "new creation" (cf. *2 Cor* 5:17), since she herself, as the first of the redeemed in salvation history, is "a new creation": she is "full of grace." It is difficult to grasp why the words of the Protoevangelium place such strong emphasis on the "woman," if it is not admitted that *in her the new and definitive Covenant* of God with humanity *has its beginning,* the *Covenant* in the redeeming blood of Christ.

The Covenant begins with a woman, the "woman" of the Annunciation at Nazareth. Herein lies the absolute originality of the Gospel: many times in the Old Testament, in order to intervene in the history of his people, God addressed himself to women, as in the case of the mothers of Samuel and Samson. However, to make his Covenant with humanity, he addressed himself only to men: *Noah, Abraham, and Moses.* At the beginning of the New Covenant, which is to be eternal and irrevocable, there is a woman: the Virgin of Nazareth. It is a sign that points to the fact that "in Jesus Christ" *"there is neither male nor female"* (Gal 3:28).In Christ the mutual opposition between man and woman — which is the inheritance of original sin — is essentially overcome. "For you are all *one* in Jesus Christ," Saint Paul will write *(ibid.).*

These words concern that original "unity of the two" which is linked with the creation of the human being as male and female, made in the image and likeness of God, and based on the model of that most perfect communion of Persons which is God himself. Saint Paul states that the mystery of man's redemption in Jesus Christ, the son of Mary, resumes and renews that which in the mystery of creation corresponded to the eternal design of God the Creator. Precisely for this reason, on the day of the creation of the human being as male and female "God saw everything that he had made, and behold, it was very good" (*Gen* 1:31). *The Redemption restores,* in a sense, at its very root, *the good* that was essentially "diminished" by sin and its heritage in human history.

The "woman" of the Proto-evangelium fits into the perspective of the Redemption. The comparison Eve-Mary can be understood also in the sense that *Mary assumes* in herself and embraces the *mystery of the "woman"* whose beginning is Eve, "the mother of all the living" (*Gen* 3:20). First of all she assumes and embraces it within the mystery of Christ, "the new and the last Adam" (cf. *1 Cor* 15:45),who assumed in his own person the nature of the first Adam. The essence of the New Covenant consists in the fact that the Son of God, who is of one substance with the eternal Father, becomes man: he takes humanity into the unity of the divine Person of the Word. The one who accomplishes the Redemption is also a true man. The mystery of the world's Redemption presupposes that *God the Son assumed humanity as the inheritance of Adam,* becoming like him and like every man in all things, "yet without sinning" (Heb 4:15). In this way he "fully reveals man to himself and makes man's supreme calling clear," as the Second Vatican Council teaches.[36] In a certain sense, he has helped man to discover "who he is" (cf. *Ps* 8:5).

In the tradition of faith and of Christian reflection throughout the ages, *the coupling Adam-Christ* is often linked with that of *Eve-Mary*. If Mary is described also as the "new Eve," what are the meanings of this analogy? Certainly there are many. Particularly noteworthy is the meaning which sees Mary as the full revelation of all that is included in the biblical word "woman": a revelation commensurate with the mystery of the Redemption. Mary means, in a sense, a going beyond the limit spoken of in the Book of Genesis (3:16) and a return to that "beginning" in which one finds the "woman" as she was intended

to be in *creation,* and therefore in the eternal mind of God: in the bosom of the Most Holy Trinity. Mary is "the new beginning" of the *dignity and vocation of women,* of each and every woman.[37]

A particular key for understanding this can be found in the words which the Evangelist puts on Mary's lips after the Annunciation, during her visit to Elizabeth: "He who is mighty has done great things for me" (*Lk* 1:49). These words certainly refer to the conception of her Son, who is the "Son of the Most High" (*Lk* 1:32), the "holy one" of God; but they can also signify *the discovery of her own feminine humanity. He "has done great things for me":* this is *the discovery of all the richness and personal resources of femininity,* all the eternal originality of the "woman," just as God wanted her to be, a person for her own sake, who discovers herself "by means of a sincere gift of self."

This discovery is connected with a clear awareness of God's gift, of his generosity. From the very "beginning" sin had obscured this awareness, in a sense had stifled it, as is shown in the words of the first temptation by the "father of lies" (cf. *Genesis* 3:1-5).At the advent of the "fullness of time" (cf. *Gal* 4:4), when the mystery of Redemption begins to be fulfilled in the history of humanity, this awareness bursts forth in all its power in the words of the biblical "woman" of Nazareth. *In Mary, Eve discovers* the nature of the true dignity of woman, of feminine humanity. This discovery must continually reach the heart of every woman and shape her vocation and her life.

QUESTIONS - Session Four

1. Having explained that man is in the "image and likeness" of God, Who is perfectly good, sin is explained as a "non-likeness," a breach in the relationship between God and creation. Sin is explained as opposition, or negation to the plan of God.

   Q. If freedom is the ability to choose the good, and sin is the abuse of that freedom, how has the modern understanding of "freedom" been so corrupted?

2. **Q. What are the consequences of Original Sin?**

3. In Genesis, after the fall from grace by Adam and Eve, God offers a foreshadowing of the ultimate victory over sin which will come about through the gift of a savior, Jesus Christ. Integral to both the fall and the restoration of the human race are women — first Eve, then Mary. In both accounts, there is reference to "the Woman."

   Q. How are Eve and Mary similar? How do they differ?

4. *"In Mary, Eve discovers* the nature of the true dignity of woman, of feminine humanity. This discovery must continually reach the heart of every woman and shape her vocation and her life" (11).

    Q. How are the following virtues exemplified by Mary in her vocation: humility; receptivity; joy; courage; and faith.

5. **Q. How does the Holy Father caution the "women's rights" movement in seeking to restore equality?**

6. **Q. Is there any hope in the face of the catastrophic sin and division spoken of in Questions 1 & 2?**

7. **Q. What is my place in this struggle? Do I make an impact in my sphere of influence?**

    A. Answers will vary.

The Importance Of Woman In The Struggle Of Good And Evil

Sin came into the world through a man and a woman. Redemption comes through a man and the free cooperation of a woman. In past ages, every covenant God made with humanity was addressed to a man (Noah, Abraham, Moses, David). It is only with the New Covenant that God restores the original harmony, the "unity of the two" by addressing a woman and awaiting her consent, her "Fiat".

> "In Christ the mutual opposition between man and woman, which is the inheritance of original sin, is essentially overcome."
> "Mary is 'the new beginning' of the dignity and vocation of women, of each and every woman."

Woman is the meeting place of God and man, both for sin and salvation. The Russian Orthodox theologian Paul Evdokimov concludes that the devil tempted Eve because she was stronger than Adam in the spiritual sphere. "When the organ most receptive and sensitive to the communion between God and man is troubled, the rest will take care of itself. Adam shows no difficulty in following Eve."[5] Mary reverses the tendency of sin by obedience to God. All women, in their own way, help to restore humanity to harmony with one another and with God.

---

[5] Paul Evdokimov, *Le Femme et le Salut du Monde*, Paris, 1958, p.157.

"They marveled that he was talking with a woman"

12. The words of the Proto-evangelium in the Book of Genesis enable us to move into the context of the Gospel. Man's Redemption, foretold in Genesis, now becomes a reality in the person and mission of Jesus Christ, in which we also recognize *what the reality of the Redemption means* for the dignity and the vocation *of women.* This meaning becomes clearer for us from Christ's words and from his whole attitude towards women, an attitude which is extremely simple, and for this very reason extraordinary, if seen against the background of his time. It is an attitude marked by great clarity and depth. Various women appear along the path of the mission of Jesus of Nazareth, and his meeting with each of them is a confirmation of the evangelical "newness of life" already spoken of.

It is universally admitted — even by people with a critical attitude towards the Christian message — that *in the eyes of his contemporaries Christ became a promoter of women's true dignity* and of the *vocation* corresponding to this dignity. At times this caused wonder, surprise, often to the point of scandal: "They marveled that he was talking with a woman" (*Jn.* 4:27), because this behavior differed from that of his contemporaries. Even Christ's own disciples "marveled." The Pharisee to whose house the sinful woman went to anoint Jesus' feet with perfumed oil "said to himself, 'If this man were a prophet, *he would have known who* and what sort of woman this is who is touching him, for she is a sinner'" (*Lk* 7:39). Even greater dismay, or even "holy indignation," must have filled the self-satisfied hearers of Christ's words: "the tax collectors and the harlots go into the Kingdom of God before you" (*Mt* 21:31).

By speaking and acting in this way, Jesus made it clear that "the mysteries of the Kingdom" were known to him in every detail. He also "knew what was in man" (*Jn.* 2:25), in his innermost being, in his "heart." He was a witness of God's eternal plan for the human being, created in his own image and likeness as man and woman. He was also perfectly aware of the consequences of sin, of that "mystery of iniquity" working in human hearts as the bitter fruit of the obscuring of the divine image. It is truly significant that in his important discussion about marriage and its indissolubility, in the presence of "the Scribes," who by profession were experts in the Law, Jesus *makes reference to the "beginning."* The question asked concerns a man's right "to divorce one's wife for any cause" (*Mt* 19:3) and therefore also concerns the woman's right, her rightful position in marriage, her dignity. The questioners think they have on their side the Mosaic legislation then followed in Israel: "Why then did Moses command one to give a certificate of divorce, and to put her away?" (*Mt* 19:7). Jesus answers: "For your hardness of heart Moses allowed you to divorce your wives, but from the beginning it was not so" (*Mt* 19:8). Jesus appeals to the "beginning," to the creation of man as male and female and their ordering by God himself, which is based upon the fact that *both were created "in his image and likeness."* Therefore, when "a man shall leave his father and mother and is joined to his wife, so that the two become one flesh," there remains in force

33

the law which comes from God himself: "What therefore God has joined together, let no man put asunder" (*Mt* 19:6).

The principle of this "ethos," which from the beginning marks the reality of creation, is now confirmed by Christ in opposition to that tradition which discriminated against women. In this tradition the male "dominated," without having proper regard for woman and for her dignity, which *the "ethos"* of creation made the basis of the mutual relationships of two people united in marriage. This "ethos" is *recalled and confirmed by Christ's words;* it is the "ethos" of the Gospel and of Redemption.

Women in the Gospel

13. As we scan the pages of the Gospel, *many women, of different ages and conditions,* pass before our eyes. We meet women with illnesses or physical sufferings, such as the one who had "a spirit of infirmity for eighteen years; she was bent over and could not fully straighten herself" (*Lk* 13:11); or Simon's mother-in-law, who "lay sick with a fever" (*Mk* 1:30); or the woman "who had a flow of blood" (cf. *Mk* 5:25-34), who could not touch anyone because it was believed that her touch would make a person "impure." Each of them was healed, and the last-mentioned — the one with a flow of blood, who touched Jesus' garment "in the crowd" (*Mk* 5:27) — was praised by him for her great faith: "Your faith has made you well" (*Mk* 5:34). Then there is *the daughter of Jairus,* whom Jesus brings back to life, saying to her tenderly: "Little girl, I say to you, arise" (*Mk* 5:41). There also is *the widow of Naim,* whose only son Jesus brings back to life, accompanying his action by an expression of affectionate mercy: "He had compassion on her and said to her, 'Do not weep!'"(*Lk* 7:13). And finally there is the *Canaanite woman,* whom Christ extols for her faith, her humility and for that greatness of spirit of which only a mother's heart is capable. "O woman, great is your faith! Be it done for you as you desire" (*Mt* 15:28). The Canaanite woman was asking for the healing of her daughter.

Sometimes the women whom Jesus met and who received so many graces from him, also accompanied him as he journeyed with the Apostles through the towns and villages, proclaiming the Good News of the Kingdom of God; and they "provided for them out of their means." The Gospel names Joanna, who was the wife of Herod's steward, Susanna and "many others" (cf. *Lk* 8:1-3).

Sometimes *women* appear *in the parables* which Jesus of Nazareth used to illustrate for his listeners the truth about the Kingdom of God. This is the case in the parables of the lost coin (cf. *Lk* 15:8-10), the leaven (cf. *Mt* 13:33), and the wise and foolish virgins (cf. *Mt* 25:1-13). Particularly eloquent is the story of the widow's mite. While "the rich were putting their gifts into the treasury. . . a poor widow put in two copper coins." Then Jesus said: "This poor widow *has put in more than all of them. . .* — she out of her poverty put in all the living that she had" (*Lk* 21:1-4). In this way Jesus presents her as a model for everyone and defends her, for in the socio-juridical system of the time widows were totally defenseless people (cf. also *Lk* 18:1-7).

In all of Jesus' teaching, as well as in his behavior, one can find nothing which reflects the discrimination against women prevalent in his day. On the contrary, *his words and works always express the respect and honor due to women.* The woman with a stoop is called a "daughter of Abraham" (*Lk* 13:16), while in the whole Bible the title "son of Abraham" is used only of men. Walking the *Via Dolorosa* to Golgotha, Jesus will say to the women: "Daughters of Jerusalem, do not weep for me" (*Lk* 23:28). This way of speaking to and about women, as well as his manner of treating them, clearly constitutes an "innovation" with respect to the prevailing custom at that time.

This becomes even more explicit in regard to women whom popular opinion contemptuously labeled sinners, public sinners and adulteresses. There is the Samaritan woman, to whom Jesus himself says: "For you have had five husbands, and he whom you now have is not your husband." And she, realizing that he knows the secrets of her life, recognizes him as the Messiah and runs to tell her neighbors. The conversation leading up to this realization is one of the most beautiful in the Gospel (cf. *Jn.* 4:7-27).

Then there is the public sinner who, in spite of her condemnation by common opinion, enters into the house of the Pharisee to anoint the feet of Jesus with perfumed oil. To his host, who is scandalized by this, he will say: "Her sins, which are many, are forgiven, for she loved much" (cf. *Lk* 7:37-47).

Finally, there is a situation which is perhaps the most eloquent: *a woman caught in adultery* is brought to Jesus. To the leading question "In the law Moses commanded us to stone such. What do you say about her?", Jesus replies: "Let him who is without sin among you be the first to throw a stone at her." The power of truth contained in this answer is so great that "they went away, one by one, beginning with the eldest." Only Jesus and the woman remain. "Woman, where are they? Has no one condemned you?" "No one, Lord." "Neither do I condemn you; go, and do not sin again" (cf. *Jn.* 8:3-11).

These episodes provide a very clear picture. Christ is the one who "knows what is in man" (cf. *Jn.* 2:25) — in man and woman. He knows *the dignity of man, his worth in God's eyes.* He himself, the Christ, is the definitive confirmation of this worth. Everything he says and does is definitively fulfilled in the Paschal Mystery of the Redemption. Jesus' attitude to the women whom he meets in the course of his Messianic service reflects the eternal plan of God, who, in creating each one of them, chooses her and loves her in Christ (cf. *Eph* 1:1-5). Each woman therefore is "the only creature on earth which God willed for its own sake." *Each of them from the "beginning" inherits as a woman the dignity of personhood.* Jesus of Nazareth confirms this dignity, recalls it, renews it, and makes it a part of the Gospel and of the Redemption for which he is sent into the world. Every word and gesture of Christ about women must therefore be brought into the dimension of the Paschal Mystery. In this way everything is completely explained.

The woman caught in adultery

14. Jesus enters *into the concrete and historical situation of women,* a situation which is *weighed down by the inheritance of sin.* One of the ways in which this inheritance is expressed is habitual discrimination against women in favor of men. This inheritance is rooted within

35

women too. From this point of view the episode of the woman "caught in adultery" (cf. *Jn.* 8:3-11) is particularly eloquent. In the end Jesus says to her: *"Do not sin again,"* but first he *evokes an awareness* of sin in the men who accuse her in order to stone her, thereby revealing his profound capacity to see human consciences and actions in their true light. Jesus seems to say to the accusers: Is not this woman, for all her sin, above all a confirmation of your own transgressions, of your "male" injustice, your misdeeds?

This truth is *valid for the whole human race.* The episode recorded in the Gospel of John is repeated in countless similar situations in every period of history. A woman is left alone, exposed to public opinion with "her sin," while behind "her" sin there lurks a man — a sinner, guilty "of the other's sin," indeed equally responsible for it. And yet his sin escapes notice, it is passed over in silence: he does not appear to be responsible for "the others's sin"! Sometimes, forgetting his own sin, he even makes himself the accuser, as in the case described. How often, in a similar way, *the woman pays* for her own sin (maybe it is she, in some cases, who is guilty of the "others's sin" — the sin of the man), but she alone pays and she pays *all alone!* How often is she abandoned with her pregnancy, when the man, the child's father, is unwilling to accept responsibility for it? And besides the many "unwed mothers" in our society, we also must consider all those who, as a result of various pressures, even on the part of the guilty man, very often "get rid of" the child before it is born. "They get rid of it": but at what price? Public opinion today tries in various ways to "abolish" the evil of this sin. Normally *a woman's conscience does not let her forget* that she has taken the life of her own child, for she cannot destroy that readiness to accept life which marks her "ethos" from the "beginning."

The attitude of Jesus in the episode described in John 8:3-11 is significant. This is one of the few instances in which his power — the power of truth — is so clearly manifested with regard to human consciences. Jesus is calm, collected and thoughtful. As in the conversation with the Pharisees (cf. *Mt* 19:3-9), is Jesus not aware of being in contact with the mystery of the "beginning," when man was created male and female, and the woman was entrusted to the man with her feminine distinctiveness, and with her potential for motherhood? The man was also entrusted by the Creator to the woman — they were *entrusted to each other as persons* made in the image and likeness of God himself. This entrusting is the test of love, spousal love. In order to become "a sincere gift" to one another, each of them has to feel responsible for the gift. This test is meant for both of them — man and woman — from the "beginning." After original sin, contrary forces are at work in man and woman as a result of the threefold concupiscence, the "stimulus of sin." They act from deep within the human being. Thus Jesus will say in the Sermon on the Mount: *"Every one who looks at a woman lustfully has already committed adultery with her in his heart"* (Mt 5:28). These words, addressed directly to man, show the fundamental truth of his responsibility vis-a-vis woman: her dignity, her motherhood, her vocation. But indirectly these words concern the woman. Christ did everything possible to ensure that — in the context of the customs and social relationships of that time — women would find in his teaching and actions their own subjectivity and dignity. On the basis of the eternal "unity of the two," *this dignity directly depends on woman herself, as a subject responsible for herself, and at the same time it is "given as a task" to man.* Christ logically appeals to man's responsibility. In the present meditation on women's dignity and vocation, it is necessary that we refer to the context which we find in the Gospel. The dignity and the vocation of women — as well as those of men — find their eternal source in the heart of God. And in the temporal conditions of human existence, they are closely connected with the "unity of the two." Consequently each man must look within himself to see whether she who was entrusted to him as a sister in humanity, as a spouse, has not become in his heart an object of adultery; to see whether she who, in different ways, is the co-subject of his existence in the world, has not become for him an "object": an object of pleasure, of exploitation.

Guardians of the Gospel message

15. *Christ's way of acting, the Gospel of his words and deeds,* is a consistent *protest* against whatever offends the dignity of women. Consequently, the women who are close to Christ discover themselves in the truth which he "teaches" and "does," even when this truth concerns their "sinfulness." They feel *"liberated" by this truth,* restored to themselves: they feel loved with "eternal love," with a love which finds direct expression in Christ himself. In Christ's sphere of action their position is transformed. They feel that Jesus is speaking to them about matters which in those times one did not discuss with a woman. Perhaps the most significant example of this is the *Samaritan woman* at the well of Sychar. *Jesus —*

who knows that she is a sinner and speaks to her about this — *discusses the most profound mysteries of God with her.* He speaks to her of God's infinite gift of love, which is like a "spring of water welling up to eternal life" (*Jn.* 4:14). He speaks to her about God who is Spirit, and about the true adoration which the Father has a right to receive in spirit and truth (cf. *Jn.* 4:24). Finally he reveals to her that he is the Messiah promised to Israel (cf. *Jn.* 4:26).

This is an event without precedent: that a *woman,* and what is more a "sinful woman," becomes a "disciple" of Christ. Indeed, once taught, she proclaims Christ to the inhabitants of Samaria, so that they too receive him with faith (cf. *Jn.* 4:39-42). This is an unprecedented event, if one remembers the usual way women were treated by those who were teachers in Israel; whereas in Jesus of Nazareth's way of acting such an event becomes normal. In this regard, the sisters of Lazarus also deserve special mention: "Jesus loved Martha and her sister (Mary) and Lazarus" (cf. *Jn.* 11:5). Mary "listened to the teaching" of Jesus: when he pays them a visit, he calls Mary's behavior "the good portion" in contrast to Martha's preoccupation with domestic matters (cf. *Lk* 10:38-42). On another occasion — *after the death of Lazarus* — Martha is the one who talks to Christ, and the conversation concerns the most profound truths of revelation and faith: "Lord, if you had been here, my brother would not have died." "Your brother will rise again." "I know that he will rise again in the resurrection at the last day." Jesus said to her: "I am the resurrection and the life; he who believes in me, though he die, yet shall he live, and whoever lives and believes in me shall never die. Do you believe this?" "Yes, Lord; I believe that you are the Christ, the Son of God, he who is coming into the world" (*Jn.* 11:21-27). After this profession of faith Jesus raises Lazarus. *This conversation with Martha is one of the most important in the Gospel.*

Christ speaks to women about the things of God, and they understand them; there is a true resonance of mind and heart, a response of faith. Jesus expresses appreciation and admiration for this distinctly "feminine" response, as in the case of the Canaanite woman (cf. *Mt* 15:28). Sometimes he presents this lively faith, filled with love, as an example. *He teaches, therefore, taking as his starting-point this feminine response of mind and heart.* This is the case with the "sinful" woman in the Pharisee's house, whose way of acting is taken by Jesus as the starting-point for explaining the truth about the forgiveness of sins: "Her sins, which are many, are forgiven, for she loved much; but he who is forgiven little, loves little" (*Lk* 7:47). On the occasion of another anointing, Jesus defends the woman and her action before the disciples, Judas in particular: "Why do you trouble this woman? *For she has done a beautiful thing to me. . . .* In pouring this ointment on my body she has done it to prepare me for burial. Truly, I say to you, wherever this gospel is preached in the whole world, what she has done will be told in memory of her" (*Mt* 26:6-13).

Indeed, the Gospels not only describe what that woman did at Bethany in the house of Simon the Leper; they also highlight the fact that *women were in the forefront at the foot of the Cross,* at the decisive moment in Jesus of Nazareth's whole messianic mission. John was the only Apostle who remained faithful, but there were many faithful women. Not only the Mother of

Christ and "his mother's sister, Mary the wife of Clopas and Mary Magdalene" (*Jn.* 19:25) were present, but "there were also many women there, looking on from afar, who had followed Jesus from Galilee, ministering to him" (*Mt* 27:55). As we see, in this most arduous test of faith and fidelity the women proved stronger than the Apostles. In this moment of danger, those who love much succeed in overcoming their fear. Before this there were the *women on the Via Dolorosa,* "who bewailed and lamented him" (*Lk* 23:27). Earlier still, there was *Pilate's wife,* who had warned her husband: "Have nothing to do with that righteous man, for I have suffered much over him today in a dream" (*Mt* 27:19).

First witnesses of the Resurrection

16. From the beginning of Christ's mission, women show to him and to his mystery a special *sensitivity which is characteristic* of their *femininity.* It must also be said that this is especially confirmed in the Paschal Mystery, not only at the Cross but also at the dawn of the Resurrection. The women *are the first at the tomb.* They are the first to find it empty. They are the first to hear: "He is not here. *He has risen,* as he said" (*Mt* 28:6). They are the first to embrace his feet (cf. *Mt* 28:9). They are also the first to be called to announce this truth to the Apostles (cf. *Mt* 28:1-10; *Lk* 24:8-11). The Gospel of John (cf. also *Mk* 16:9) *emphasizes the special role of Mary Magdalene.* She is the first to meet the Risen Christ. At first she thinks he is the gardener; she recognizes him only when he calls her by name: "Jesus said to her, 'Mary.' She turned and said to him in Hebrew, 'Rabbuni' (which means Teacher). Jesus said to her, 'Do not hold

me, for I have not yet ascended to the Father, but go to my brethren and say to them, I am ascending to my Father and to your Father, to my God and your God.' Mary Magdalene went and said to the disciples, 'I have seen the Lord'; and she told them that he had said these things to her" (*Jn.* 20:16-18).

Hence she came to be called "the apostle of the Apostles."[38] Mary Magdalene was the first eyewitness of the Risen Christ, and for this reason she was also *the first to bear witness to him before the Apostles.* This event, in a sense, crowns all that has been said previously about Christ entrusting divine truths to women as well as men. One can say that this fulfilled the words of the Prophet: *"I will pour out my spirit on all flesh;* your sons and *your daughters shall prophesy"* (Jl 3:1). On the fiftieth day after Christ's Resurrection, these words are confirmed once more in the Upper Room in Jerusalem, at the descent of the Holy Spirit, the Paraclete (cf. Act 2:17).

Everything that has been said so far about Christ's attitude to women confirms and clarifies, in the Holy Spirit, the truth about the equality of man and woman. One must speak of an essential "equality," since both of them — the woman as much as the man — are created in the image and likeness of God. Both of them are equally capable of receiving the outpouring of divine truth and love in the Holy Spirit. Both receive his salvific and sanctifying "visits."

The fact of being a man or a woman involves no limitation here, just as the salvific and sanctifying action of the Spirit in man is in no way limited by the fact that one is a Jew or a Greek, slave or free, according to the well-known words of Saint Paul: "For you are all one in Christ Jesus" (Gal 3:28). *This unity does not cancel out diversity.* The Holy Spirit, who brings about this unity in the supernatural order of sanctifying grace, contributes in equal measure to the fact that "your sons will prophesy" and that "your daughters will prophesy." "To prophesy" means to express by one's words and one's life *"the mighty works of God"* (*Acts* 2:11), preserving the truth and originality of each person, whether woman or man. Gospel "equality," the "equality" of women and men in regard to the "mighty works of God" — manifested so clearly in the words and deeds of Jesus of Nazareth — constitutes the most obvious basis for the dignity and vocation of women in the Church and in the world. Every *vocation has* a profoundly *personal and prophetic meaning.* In "vocation" understood in this way, what is personally feminine reaches a new dimension: the dimension of the "mighty works of God," of which the woman becomes the living subject and an irreplaceable witness.

QUESTIONS - Session Five

1. This session recalls women in the New Testament. It reflects upon the relationships Jesus had with women and what we can learn from them about the dignity and vocation of women.

    Q. **In what ways did Jesus' attitude toward women reveal that the traditions operate contrary to the "ethos" of creation?**

2. Q. **Which are the key messages of the meeting of Jesus with the woman caught in adultery? (14; *Jn.* 8:3-11)**

3. Q. **What are some important points in the encounter between Jesus and the Samaritan woman? (15; *Jn.* 4:39-42)**

4. Q. **Considering the story of the Samaritan woman, do you see a pattern similar to Christ's other encounters with women?**

5. Q. **Why is Jesus' conversation with Martha in *Jn.* 11:21-27 "one of the most important in the Gospels"?**

6. Q. What feminine quality does Mary Magdalene reveal at the Resurrection?

7. Q. What are some of the ways the Spirit at Pentecost confirms the equality of men and women?

8. Q. Do you find yourself relating to any of the women in the Gospels? In what way?

9. Pope John Paul II was himself the greatest and most visible prophet in recent history along with the life testimony of Blessed Mother Teresa. However, we are all called to be prophets within our own families and communities. We must stand for the truth — witness to it — through our words and actions.
   Q. Who do you know in your own communities who are doing this in a heroic way? How can you also be a more effective prophet?

Two Dimensions of Women's Vocation

17. We must now focus our meditation on virginity and motherhood as two particular dimensions of the fulfillment of the female personality. In the light of the Gospel, they acquire their full meaning and value in Mary, who as a Virgin became the Mother of the Son of God. These *two dimensions of the female vocation* were united in her in an exceptional manner, in such a way that one did not exclude the other but wonderfully complemented it. The description of the Annunciation in the Gospel of Luke clearly shows that this seemed impossible to the Virgin of Nazareth. When she hears the words: "You will conceive in your womb and bear a son, and you shall call his name Jesus," she immediately asks: "How can this be, since I have no husband?" (*Lk* 1:31,34). In the usual order of things motherhood is the result of mutual "knowledge" between a man and woman in the marriage union. Mary, firm in her resolve to preserve her virginity, puts this question to the divine messenger, and obtains from him the explanation: *"The Holy Spirit will come upon you"* — your motherhood will not be the consequence of matrimonial "knowledge," but will be the work of the Holy Spirit; the "power of the Most High" will "overshadow" the mystery of the Son's conception and birth; as the Son of the Most High, he is given to you exclusively by God, in a manner known to God. Mary, therefore, maintained her virginal "I have no husband" (cf. *Lk* 1:34) and at the same time became a Mother. *Virginity and motherhood co-exist in her:* they do not mutually exclude each other or place limits on each other. Indeed, the person of the Mother of God helps everyone — especially women — to see how these two dimensions, these two paths in the vocation of women as persons, explain and complete each other.

Motherhood

18. In order to share in this "vision," we must once again *seek a deeper understanding of the truth about the human person* recalled by the Second Vatican Council. The human being — both male and female — is the only being in the world which God willed for its own sake. The human being is a person, a subject who decides for himself. At the same time, man "cannot fully find himself except through a sincere gift of self."[39] It has already been said that this description, indeed this definition of the person, corresponds to the fundamental biblical truth about the creation of the human being — man and woman — in the image and likeness of God. This is not a purely theoretical interpretation, nor an abstract definition, for *it gives an essential indication of what it means to be human,* while emphasizing *the value of the gift of self, the gift of the person.* In this vision of the person we also find the essence of that "ethos" which, together with the truth of creation, will be fully developed by the books of Revelation, particularly the Gospels.

This truth about the person also opens up *the path to a full understanding of women's motherhood.* Motherhood is the fruit of the marriage union of a man and woman, of that biblical "knowledge" which corresponds to the "union of the two in one flesh" (cf. *Gen* 2:24). This brings about — on the woman's part — a special "gift of self," as an expression of that spousal love whereby the two are united to each other so closely that they become "one flesh." Biblical "knowledge" is achieved in accordance with the truth of the person only when the mutual self-giving is not distorted either by the desire of the man to become the "master" of his wife ("he shall rule over you") or by the woman remaining closed within her own instincts ("your desire shall be for your husband": *Gen* 3:16).

This *mutual gift of the person in marriage* opens to the gift of a new life, *a new human being,* who is also a person in the likeness of his parents. Motherhood implies from the beginning a special openness to the new person: and this is precisely the woman's "part." In this openness, in conceiving and giving birth to a child, the woman "discovers herself through a sincere gift of self." The gift of interior readiness to accept the child and bring it into the world is linked to the marriage union, which — as mentioned earlier — should constitute a special moment in the mutual self-giving both by the woman and the man. According to the Bible, the conception and birth of a new human being are accompanied by the following words of the woman: *"I have brought a man into being with the help of the Lord" (Gen* 4:1).This exclamation of Eve, the "mother of all the living" is repeated every time a new human being comes into the world. It expresses the woman's joy and awareness that she is sharing in the great mystery of eternal generation. The spouses share in the creative power of God!

The woman's motherhood in the period between the baby's conception and birth is a bio-physiological and psychological process which is better understood in our days than in the past, and is the subject of many detailed studies. Scientific analysis fully confirms that the very physical constitution of women is naturally disposed to motherhood — conception, pregnancy and giving birth — which is a consequence of the marriage union with the man. At the same time, this also corresponds to the psycho-physical structure of women. What the different branches of science have to say on this subject is important and useful, provided that it is not limited to an exclusively bio-physiological interpretation of women and of motherhood. Such a *"restricted" picture* would go hand in hand with a materialistic concept of the human being and of the world. In such a case, what is truly essential would unfortunately be lost. Motherhood as a human fact and phenomenon, is fully explained on the basis of the truth about the person. Motherhood *is linked to the personal structure of the woman and to the personal dimension of the gift:* "I have brought a man into being with the help of the Lord" (*Gen* 4:1). The Creator grants the parents the gift of a child. On the woman's part, this fact is linked in a special way to "a sincere gift of self." Mary's words at the Annunciation — "Let it be to me according to your word" — signify the woman's readiness for the gift of self and her readiness to accept a new life.

The eternal mystery of generation, which is in God himself, the one and Triune God (cf. *Eph* 3:14-15), is reflected in the woman's motherhood and in the man's fatherhood. Human parenthood is something shared by both the man and the woman. Even if the woman, out of love for her husband, says: "I have given you a child," her words also mean: "This is our child." Although both of them together are parents of their child, *the woman's motherhood constitutes a special "part" in this shared parenthood,* and the most demanding part. Parenthood — even though it belongs to both — is realized much more fully in the woman, especially in the prenatal period. It is the woman who "pays" directly for this shared generation, which literally absorbs the energies of her body and soul. It is therefore necessary that *the man* be fully aware that in their shared parenthood he owes *a special debt to the woman.* No programme of "equal rights" between women and men is valid unless it takes this fact fully into account.

Motherhood involves a special communion with the mystery of life, as it develops in the woman's womb. The mother is filled with wonder at this mystery of life, and "understands" with unique intuition what is happening inside her. In the light of the "beginning," the mother accepts and loves as a person the child she is carrying in her womb. This unique contact with the new human being developing within her gives rise to an attitude towards human beings - not only towards her own child, but every human being — which profoundly marks the woman's personality. It is commonly thought that women are more capable than men of paying attention to another person, and that motherhood develops this predisposition even more. The man — even with all his sharing in parenthood — always remains "outside" the process of pregnancy and the baby's birth; in many ways he has to *learn* his own *"fatherhood" from the mother.* One can say that this is part of the normal human dimension of parenthood, including the stages that follow the birth of the baby, especially the initial period. The child's upbringing, taken as a whole, should include the contribution of both parents: the maternal and paternal contribution. In any event, the mother's contribution is decisive in laying the foundation for a new human personality.

Motherhood in relation to the Covenant

19. Our reflection returns to *the biblical exemplar of the "woman"* in the Proto-evangelium. The "woman," as mother and first teacher of the human being (education being the spiritual dimension of parenthood), has a specific precedence over the man. Although motherhood, especially *in the bio-physical sense,* depends upon the man, it places an essential "mark" on the whole personal growth process of new children. Motherhood in the bio-physical sense appears to be passive: the formation process of a new life "takes place" in her, in her body, which is nevertheless profoundly involved in that process. At the same time, motherhood *in its personal-ethical sense* expresses a very important creativity on the part of the woman, upon whom the very humanity of the new human being mainly depends. In this sense too the woman's motherhood presents a special call and a special challenge to the man and to his fatherhood.

The biblical exemplar of the "woman" finds its culmination *in the motherhood of the Mother of God.* The words of the Proto-evangelium — "I will put enmity between you and the woman" — find here a fresh confirmation. We see that through Mary — through her maternal "fiat," ("Let it be done to me") — God *begins a New Covenant with humanity.* This is the eternal and definitive Covenant in Christ, in his body and blood, in his Cross and Resurrection. Precisely because this Covenant is to be fulfilled "in flesh and blood" its beginning is in the Mother. Thanks solely to her and to her virginal and maternal "fiat," the "Son of the Most High" can say to the Father: "A body you have prepared for me. Lo, I have come to do your will, O God" (cf. *Heb* 10:5,7).

Motherhood has been introduced into the order of the Covenant that God made with humanity in Jesus Christ. Each and every time that *motherhood* is repeated in human history, it is always *related to the Covenant* which God established with the human race through the motherhood of the Mother of God.

Does not Jesus bear witness to this reality when he answers the exclamation of that woman in the crowd who blessed him for Mary's motherhood: "Blessed is the womb that bore you, and the breasts that you sucked!"? Jesus replies: "Blessed rather are those who hear the word of God and keep it" (*Lk* 11:27-28). Jesus confirms the meaning of motherhood in reference to the body, but at the same time he indicates an even deeper meaning, which is connected with the order of the spirit: it is a sign of the Covenant with God who "is spirit" (*Jn.* 4:24). This is true above all for the motherhood of the Mother of God. *The motherhood* of every woman, understood in the light of the Gospel, is similarly not only "of flesh and blood": it expresses a profound *"listening to the word of the living God"* and a readiness to "safeguard" this Word, which is "the word of eternal life" (cf. *Jn.* 6:68). For it is precisely those born of earthly mothers, the sons and daughters of the human race, who receive from the Son of God the power to become "children of God" (*Jn.* 1:12). A dimension of the New Covenant in Christ's blood enters into human parenthood, making it a reality and a task for "new

creatures" (cf. *2 Cor* 5:17). The history of every human being passes through the threshold of a woman's motherhood; crossing it conditions "the revelation of the children of God" (cf. *Rom* 8:19).

"When a woman is in travail she has sorrow, because her hour has come; but when she is delivered of the child, *she no longer remembers the anguish,* for joy that a child is born into the world" (*Jn.* 16:21). The first part of Christ's words refers to the "pangs of childbirth" which belong to the heritage of original sin; at the same time these words indicate *the link that exists between the woman's motherhood and the Paschal Mystery.* For this mystery also includes the Mother's sorrow at the foot of the Cross — the Mother who through faith shares in the amazing mystery of her Son's "self-emptying": "This is perhaps the deepest 'kenosis' of faith in human history."[40]

As we contemplate this Mother, whose heart "a sword has pierced" (cf. *Lk* 2:35), our thoughts go to *all the suffering women in the world,* suffering either physically or morally. In this suffering a woman's sensitivity plays a role, even though she often succeeds in resisting suffering better than a man. It is difficult to enumerate these sufferings; it is difficult to call them all by name. We may recall her maternal care for her children, especially when they fall sick or fall into bad ways; the death of those most dear to her; the loneliness of mothers forgotten by their grown up children; the loneliness of widows; the sufferings of women who struggle alone to make a living; and women who have been wronged or exploited. Then there are the sufferings of consciences as a result of sin, which has wounded the woman's human or maternal dignity: the wounds of consciences which do not heal easily. With these sufferings too we must place ourselves at the foot of the Cross.

But the words of the Gospel about the woman who suffers when the time comes for her to give birth to her child, immediately afterwards express joy: it is *"the joy that a child is born into the world."* This joy too is referred to the Paschal Mystery, to the joy which is communicated to the Apostles *on the day of Christ's Resurrection:* "So you have sorrow now" (these words were said the day before the Passion); "but I will see you again and your hearts will rejoice, and no one will take your joy from you" (*Jn.* 16:22-23).

QUESTIONS - Session Six

1. "In order to share in this 'vision' [the true vocation of women], we must . . . seek a deeper understanding of the truth about the human person" (*MD*, 18).

   Q. How does the Pope define the human person?

2. **Q. Why is openness to persons an important quality for woman and motherhood?**

3. The Pope clearly explains how "the woman's motherhood constitutes a special 'part' in our shared parenthood." The woman "pays" dearly and directly for new life, "which literally absorbs the energies of her body and soul." Hence, the man owes her a special debt of gratitude and respect. The Holy Father further states, "The man — even with all his sharing in parenthood — always remains 'outside' the process of pregnancy and the baby's birth; in many ways he has to learn his own 'fatherhood' from the mother." Parents must work together, but it is the mother who lays the foundation for family and forms a new personality in the child (*MD*, 18, paragraph 6).

   Q. How is a woman's attitude towards men, beginning with her own husband, indicative of how he is received within the family? His circle?

4. **Q. How can we combat the ubiquitous negative image of men in the media?**

5. Q. Can you give examples of women who have paid a "high price" for their children? Or men who have been keenly aware of sacrifices made by their wives?

6. Q. How does motherhood make a woman more attentive to other people in general? Do you have personal experiences to share?

7. Q. How does the motherhood of every woman share in the New Covenant of Christ's death and resurrection? What does this mean in my life?

8. Discuss how women share in the Paschal Mystery.

See Supplement, *Understanding Women*

"Understanding Women"

It is commonly observed that women often endure suffering better than men. Men tend to deny pain. Women are emotionally healthier to confront pain, bear it and make something positive out of it. Carry pain as did the Blessed Virgin at the foot of the cross. If your husband doesn't understand you, don't complain; rather, understand him and see the healing that takes place within your heart and in his attitude. Don't whine or become a victim, but deal with problems and become a true feminine leader in your home and community. (It is good to note that if a wife is affirming to her husband, his son will feel good about himself; and if a father is affirming to the wife, the daughter will feel good about herself.)

Women work and lead intuitively. Like Mary at Cana, they skillfully arrange conditions so something can happen. Of course there are exceptions, but in general this is the predominant feminine method of action. Women also tend to take things in and ponder them. (It may come out later.) Think of Mary, finding Jesus in the temple after three days, who "kept all these things in her heart." Boys tend to be *intrusive,* going out into space, building towers and taking charge of things outside of their immediate space. Girls, on the other hand, are more *inclusive,* drawing others into a group or into their heart, building enclosures and staying more "in body." Women can go out and be lawyers, etc., but the predominance is inclusive. In the case of Edith Stein, her masculine attitude was fuelling her femininity. Pope John Paul II is a giant of a man but he also has great sensitivity. He is masculine first and then spiritual. Develop your feminine leadership abilities and you will be happier and more effective in your endeavors.

Virginity for the Sake of the Kingdom

20. In the teaching of Christ, *motherhood is connected with virginity,* but also *distinct from it.* Fundamental to this is Jesus' statement in the conversation on the indissolubility of marriage. Having heard the answer given to the Pharisees, the disciples say to Christ: "If such is the case of a man with his wife, it is not expedient to marry" (*Mt* 19:10). Independently of the meaning which "it is not expedient" had at that time in the mind of the disciples, Christ takes their mistaken opinion as a starting point for instructing them on the value of celibacy. He distinguishes celibacy which results from natural defects — even though they may have been caused by man — from *"celibacy for the sake of the Kingdom of heaven."* Christ says, "and there are eunuchs who have made themselves eunuchs for the sake of the Kingdom of heaven" (*Mt* 19:12). It is, then, a voluntary celibacy, chosen for the sake of the Kingdom of heaven, in view of man's eschatological vocation to union with God. He then adds: "He who is able to receive this, let him receive it." These words repeat what he had said at the beginning of the discourse on celibacy (cf. *Mt* 19:11). Consequently, *celibacy for the kingdom of heaven* results not only from a free *choice* on the part of man, but also from a special grace on the part of God, who calls a particular person to live celibacy. While this is a special sign of the Kingdom of God to come, it also serves as a way to devote all the energies of soul and body during one's earthly life exclusively for the sake of the eschatological kingdom.

Jesus' words are the answer to the disciples' question. They are addressed directly to those who put the question: in this case they were men. Nevertheless, Christ's answer, in itself, has a *value both for men and for women.* In this context it indicates the evangelical ideal of virginity, an ideal which constitutes a clear "innovation" with respect to the tradition of the Old Testament. Certainly that tradition was connected in some way with Israel's expectation of the Messiah's coming, especially among the women of Israel from whom he was to be born. In fact, the ideal of celibacy and virginity for the sake of greater closeness to God was not entirely foreign to certain Jewish circles, especially in the period immediately preceding the coming of Jesus. Nevertheless, celibacy for the sake of the Kingdom, or rather virginity, is undeniably an innovation connected with the incarnation of God.

From the moment of Christ's coming, the expectation of the People of God has to be directed to the eschatological Kingdom which is coming and to which he must lead "the new Israel." A new awareness of faith is essential for such a turn-about and change of values. Christ emphasizes this twice: "He who is able to receive this, let him receive it." Only "those to whom it is given" understand it (*Mt* 19:11). *Mary* is the first person in whom this *new awareness* is manifested, for she asks the Angel: "How can this be, since I have no husband?" (*Lk* 1:34).Even though she is "betrothed to a man whose name was Joseph" (cf. *Lk* 1:27), she is firm in her resolve to remain a virgin. The motherhood which is accomplished in her comes exclusively from the "power of the Most High," and is the result of the Holy Spirit's coming down upon her (cf. *Lk* 1:35). This divine motherhood, therefore,

51

is an altogether unforeseen response to the human expectation of women in Israel: it comes to Mary as a gift from God himself. This gift is the beginning and the prototype of a new expectation on the part of all. It measures up to the Eternal Covenant, to God's new and definitive promise: it is *a sign of eschatological hope.*

On the basis of the Gospel, the meaning of virginity was developed and better understood as a vocation for women too, one in which their dignity, like that of the Virgin of Nazareth, finds confirmation. The Gospel puts forward *the ideal of the consecration of the person,* that is, the person's exclusive dedication to God by virtue of the evangelical counsels: in particular, chastity, poverty and obedience. Their perfect incarnation is Jesus Christ himself. Whoever wishes to follow him in a radical way chooses to live according to these counsels. They are distinct from the commandments and show the Christian the radical way of the Gospel. From the very beginning of Christianity men and women have set out on this path, since the evangelical ideal is addressed to human beings without any distinction of sex.

In this wider context, *virginity* has to be considered *also as a path for women,* a path on which they realize their womanhood in a way different from marriage. In order to understand this path, it is necessary to refer once more to the fundamental idea of Christian anthropology. By freely choosing virginity, women confirm themselves as persons, as beings whom the Creator from the beginning has willed for their own sake.[41] At the same time they realize the personal value of their own femininity by becoming "a sincere gift" for God who has revealed himself in Christ, a gift for Christ, the Redeemer of humanity and the Spouse

of souls: a "spousal" gift. *One cannot correctly understand virginity* — a woman's consecration in virginity — *without referring to spousal love.* It is through this kind of love that a person becomes a gift for the other.[42] Moreover, a man's consecration in priestly celibacy or in the religious state is to be understood analogously.

The naturally spousal predisposition of the feminine personality finds a response in virginity understood in this way. Women, called from the very "beginning" to be loved and to love, in a vocation to virginity *find Christ* first of all as the Redeemer who "loved until the end" through his total gift of self; *and they respond to this gift with a "sincere gift"* of their whole lives. They thus give themselves to the divine Spouse, and this personal gift tends to union, which is properly spiritual in character. Through the Holy Spirit's action a woman becomes "one spirit" with Christ the Spouse (cf. *1 Cor* 6:17).

This is the evangelical ideal of virginity, in which both the dignity and the vocation of women are realized in a special way. In virginity thus understood the so-called *radicalism of the Gospel* finds expression: "Leave everything and follow Christ" (cf. *Mt* 19:27). This cannot be compared to remaining simply unmarried or single, because virginity is not restricted to a mere "no," but contains a profound "yes" in the spousal order: the gift of self for love in a total and undivided manner.

Motherhood according to the Spirit

21. Virginity according to the Gospel means *renouncing marriage and thus physical motherhood.* Nevertheless, the renunciation of this kind of motherhood, a

renunciation that can involve great sacrifice for a woman, makes possible a different kind of motherhood: motherhood *"according to the Spirit"* (cf. *Rom* 8:4). For virginity does not deprive a woman of her prerogatives. Spiritual motherhood takes on many different forms. In the life of consecrated women, for example, who live according to the charism and the rules of the various Apostolic Institutes, it can express itself as concern for people, especially the most needy: the sick, the handicapped, the abandoned, orphans, the elderly, children, young people, the imprisoned and, in general, people on the edges of society. *In this way a consecrated woman finds her Spouse,* different and the same in each and every person, according to his very words: "As you did it to one of the least of these my brethren, you did it to me" (*Mt* 25:40). Spousal love always involves a special readiness to be poured out for the sake of those who come within one's range of activity. In marriage this readiness, even though open to all, consists mainly in the love that parents give to their children. In virginity this readiness is open *to all people, who are embraced by the love of Christ the Spouse.*

Spousal love — with its maternal potential hidden in the heart of the woman as a virginal bride — when joined to Christ, the Redeemer of each and every person, is also predisposed to being open to each and every person. This is confirmed in the religious communities of apostolic life, and in a different way in communities of contemplative life, or the cloister. There exist still other forms of a vocation to virginity for the sake of the Kingdom; for example, the Secular Institutes, or the communities of consecrated persons which flourish within Movements, Groups and Associations. In all of these *the same truth*

about the spiritual motherhood of virgins is confirmed in various ways. However, it is not only a matter of communal forms but also of non-communal forms. In brief, virginity as a woman's vocation is always the vocation of a person — of a unique, individual person. Therefore the spiritual motherhood which makes itself felt in this vocation is also profoundly personal.

This is also the basis of a specific *convergence between the virginity* of the unmarried woman and *the motherhood* of the married woman. This convergence moves not only from motherhood towards virginity, as emphasized above; it also moves from virginity towards marriage, the form of woman's vocation in which she becomes a mother by giving birth to her children. The starting point of this second analogy is *the meaning of marriage.* A woman is "married" either through the sacrament of marriage or spiritually through marriage to Christ. In both cases marriage signifies the "sincere gift of the person" of the bride to the groom. In this way, one can say that the profile of marriage is found spiritually in virginity. And does not physical motherhood also have to be a spiritual motherhood, in order to respond to the whole truth about the human being who is a unity of body and spirit? Thus there exist many reasons for discerning in these two different paths — the two different vocations of women — a profound complementarity, and even a profound union within a person's being.

"My little children with whom I am again in travail"

22. The Gospel reveals and enables us to understand precisely this *mode of being of the human person.* The Gospel helps every woman and every man to live it and thus attain fulfilment. There exists a total

equality with respect to the gifts of the Holy Spirit, with respect to the "mighty works of God" (*Acts* 2:11). Moreover, it is precisely in the face of the "mighty works of God" that Saint Paul, as a man, feels the need to refer to what is essentially feminine in order to express the truth about his own apostolic service. This is exactly what Paul of Tarsus does when he addresses the Galatians with the words: *"My little children, with whom I am again in travail"* (*Gal* 4:19). In the First Letter to the Corinthians (7:38) Saint Paul proclaims the superiority of virginity over marriage, which is a constant teaching of the Church in accordance with the spirit of Christ's words recorded in the Gospel of Matthew (19:10-12); he does so without in any way obscuring the importance of physical and spiritual motherhood. Indeed, in order to illustrate the Church's fundamental mission, he finds nothing better than the reference to motherhood.

The same analogy — and the same truth — are present in the Dogmatic Constitution on the Church. *Mary is the "figure" of the Church*:[43] "For in the mystery of the Church, herself rightly called mother and virgin, the Blessed Virgin came first as an eminent and singular exemplar of both virginity and motherhood. . . . The Son whom she brought forth is He whom God placed as the first-born among many brethren (cf. *Rom* 8:29), namely, among the faithful. In their birth and development she cooperates with a maternal love."[44] "Moreover, contemplating Mary's mysterious sanctity, imitating her charity, and faithfully fulfilling the Father's will, the Church *herself becomes a mother* by accepting God's word in faith. For by her preaching and by baptism she brings forth to a new and immortal life children who are conceived by the Holy Spirit and born of God."[45] This is motherhood "according to the Spirit" with regard to the sons and daughters of the human race. And this motherhood — as already mentioned — becomes the woman's "role" also in virginity "The Church *herself is a virgin,* who keeps whole and pure the fidelity she has pledged to her Spouse."[46] This is most perfectly fulfilled in Mary. The Church, therefore, "imitating the Mother of her Lord, and by the power of the Holy Spirit, . . . preserves with virginal purity an integral faith, a firm hope, and a sincere charity."[47]

The Council has confirmed that, unless one looks to the Mother of God, it is impossible to understand the mystery of the Church, her reality, her essential vitality. *Indirectly* we find here *a reference* to the *biblical exemplar of the "woman"* which is already clearly outlined in the description of the "beginning" (cf. *Gen* 3:15) and which proceeds from creation, through sin to the Redemption. In this way there is a confirmation of the profound union between what is human and what constitutes the divine economy of salvation in human history. The Bible convinces us of the fact that one can have no adequate hermeneutic of man, or of what is "human," without appropriate reference to what is "feminine." There is an analogy in God's salvific economy: if we wish to understand it fully in relation to the whole of human history, we cannot omit, in the perspective of our faith, the mystery of "woman": virgin-mother-spouse.

QUESTIONS - Session Seven

1. Jesus describes "a voluntary celibacy, chosen for the sake of the Kingdom of heaven, in view of man's eschatological vocation to union with God." This comes not only from the choice of the individual but by means of a special grace from God as part of the call.

   Q. What are the two most important aspects of the celibate vocation?

2. The Pope writes, "In the teaching of Christ, motherhood is connected with virginity, but also distinct from it."

   Q. What are some of the similarities and some of the differences of these two vocations?

3. **Q. How can a woman dedicated to God by the vow of chastity exercise her full personhood?**

4. **Q. How do the evangelical counsels of consecrated life (poverty, chastity, and obedience) each provide a means of witnessing to the larger world that has forgotten God to a large extent?**

5. Q. Does this explanation of virginity help to understand why the Church values celibacy for priests?

6. Q. What are some practical ways to show support for those who are called to embrace the evangelical counsels? Where are these men and women found in your local area?

The "Great Mystery"

23. Of fundamental importance here are the words of the Letter to the Ephesians: "Husbands, love your wives, as Christ loved the Church and gave himself up for her, that he might sanctify her, having cleansed her by the washing of water with the word, that he might present the Church to himself in splendor, without spot or wrinkle or any such thing, that she might be holy and without blemish. Even so husbands should love their wives as their own bodies. He who loves his wife loves himself. For no man ever hates his own flesh, but nourishes and cherishes it, as Christ does the Church, because we are members of his body. 'For this reason a man shall leave his father and mother and be joined to his wife, and the two shall become one flesh.' *This mystery is a profound one,* and I am saying that *it refers to Christ and the Church*" (5:25-32).

In this Letter the author expresses the truth about the Church as the bride of Christ, and also indicates how this truth *is rooted in the biblical reality of the creation of the human being as male and female.* Created in the image and likeness of God as a "unity of the two," both have been called to a spousal love. Following the description of creation in the Book of Genesis (2:18-25), one can also say that this fundamental call appears in the creation of woman, and is inscribed by the Creator in the institution of marriage, which, according to Genesis 2:24, has the character of a union of persons *("communio personarum")* from the very beginning. Although not directly, the very description of the "beginning" (cf. *Gen* 1:27; 2:24) shows that the whole "ethos"

of mutual relations between men and women has to correspond to the personal truth of their being.

All this has already been considered. The Letter to the Ephesians once again confirms this truth, while at the same time comparing the spousal character of the love between man and woman to the mystery of Christ and of the Church. *Christ is the Bridegroom of the Church - the Church is the Bride of Christ.* This analogy is not without precedent; it transfers to the New Testament what was already contained *in the Old Testament,* especially in the prophets Hosea, Jeremiah, Ezekiel and Isaiah.[48] The respective passages deserve a separate analysis. Here we will cite only one text. This is how God speaks to his Chosen People through the Prophet: "Fear not, for you will not be ashamed; be not confounded, for you will not be put to shame; for you will forget the shame of your youth, and the reproach of your widowhood you will remember no more. *For your Maker is your husband,* the Lord of hosts is his name; and the Holy One of Israel is *your Redeemer,* the God of the whole earth he is called. For the Lord has called you like a wife forsaken and grieved in spirit, like a wife of youth when she is cast off, says your God. For a brief moment I forsook you, but with great compassion I will gather you. In overflowing wrath for a moment I hid my face from you, but with everlasting love I will have compassion on you, says the Lord, your Redeemer. . . . For the mountains may depart and the hills be removed, *but my steadfast love shall not depart from you,* and my covenant of peace shall not be removed, says the Lord, who has compassion on you" (*Is* 54:4-8, 10).

Since the human being — man and woman — has been created in God's image and likeness, God can speak about himself through the lips of the Prophet using language which is essentially human. In the text of Isaiah quoted above, the expression of God's love is *"human,"* but the *love* itself *is divine.* Since it is God's love, its spousal character is properly divine, even though it is expressed by the analogy of a man's love for a woman. The woman-bride is Israel, God's Chosen People, and this choice originates exclusively in God's gratuitous love. It is precisely this love which explains the Covenant, a Covenant often presented as a marriage covenant which God always renews with his Chosen People. On the part of God the Covenant is a lasting "commitment"; he remains faithful to his spousal love even if the bride often shows herself to be unfaithful.

This *image of spousal love,* together with the figure of the divine Bridegroom — a very clear image in the texts of the Prophets — finds crowning confirmation in the Letter to the Ephesians (5:23-32). *Christ* is greeted as the bridegroom by John the Baptist (cf. *Jn.* 3:27-29). Indeed Christ applies to himself this comparison drawn from the Prophets (cf. *Mk* 2:19-20). The Apostle Paul, who is a bearer of the Old Testament heritage, writes to the Corinthians: "I feel a divine jealousy for you, for I betrothed you to Christ to present you as a pure bride to her one husband" (*2 Cor* 11:2). But the fullest expression of the truth about Christ the Redeemer's love, according to the analogy of spousal love in marriage, is found in the Letter to the Ephesians: *"Christ loved the Church and gave himself up for her"* (5:25), thereby fully confirming the fact that the Church is the bride of Christ: "The Holy One of Israel is your Redeemer" (*Is* 54:5). In Saint Paul's text the analogy of the spousal relationship moves simultaneously in two directions which make up the whole of the "great mystery" *("sacramentum magnum").*

The covenant proper to spouses "explains" the spousal character of the union of Christ with the Church, and in its turn this union, as a "great sacrament," determines the sacramentality of marriage as a holy covenant between the two spouses, man and woman. Reading this rich and complex passage, which *taken as a whole is a great analogy,* we must *distinguish* that element which expresses the human reality of interpersonal relations from that which expresses in symbolic language the "great mystery" which is divine.

The Gospel "Innovation"

24. The text is addressed to the spouses as real women and men. It reminds them of the "ethos" of spousal love which goes back to the divine institution of marriage from the "beginning." Corresponding to the truth of this institution is the exhortation: *"Husbands, love your wives,"* love them because of that special and unique bond whereby in marriage a man and a woman become "one flesh" (*Gen* 2:24; *Eph* 5:31). In this love there is a fundamental *affirmation of the woman* as a person. This affirmation makes it possible for the female personality to develop fully and be enriched. This is precisely the way Christ acts as the bridegroom of the Church; he desires that she be "in splendor, without spot or wrinkle" (*Eph* 5:27). One can say that this fully captures the whole "style" of Christ in dealing with women. Husbands should make their own the elements of this style in regard to their

wives; analogously, all men should do the same in regard to women in every situation. In this way both men and women bring about "the sincere gift of self."

The author of the Letter to the Ephesians sees no contradiction between an exhortation formulated in this way and the words: "Wives, be subject to your husbands, as to the Lord. For the husband is the head of the wife" (5:22-23). The author knows that this way of speaking, so profoundly rooted in the customs and religious tradition of the time, is to be understood and carried out in a new way: as a *mutual subjection out of reverence for Christ*" (cf. *Eph* 5:21). This is especially true because the husband is called the "head" of the wife as Christ is the head of the Church; he is so in order to give "himself up for her" (*Eph* 5:25), and giving himself up for her means giving up even his own life. However, whereas in the relationship between Christ and the Church the subjection is only on the part of the Church, in the relationship between husband and wife the "subjection" is not one-sided but mutual.

In relation to the "old" this is evidently something "new": it is an innovation of the Gospel. We find various passages in which the apostolic writings express this innovation, even though they also communicate what is "old": what is rooted in the religious tradition of Israel, in its way of understanding and explaining the sacred texts, as for example the second chapter of the Book of Genesis.[49]

The apostolic letters are addressed to people living in an environment marked by that same traditional way of thinking and acting. The "innovation" of Christ is a fact: it constitutes the unambiguous content of the evangelical message and is the result of the Redemption. However, the awareness that in marriage there is mutual "subjection of the spouses out of reverence for Christ," and not just that of the wife to the husband, must gradually establish itself in hearts, consciences, behavior and customs. This is a call which from that time onwards, does not cease to challenge succeeding generations; it is a call which people have to accept ever anew. Saint Paul not only wrote: "In Christ Jesus… there is no more man or woman," but also wrote: "There is no more slave or freeman." Yet how many generations were needed for such a principle to be realized in the history of humanity through the abolition of slavery! And what is one to say of the many forms of slavery to which individuals and peoples are subjected, which have not yet disappeared from history?

But *the challenge presented by the "ethos" of the Redemption* is clear and definitive. All the reasons in favor of the "subjection" of woman to man in marriage must be understood in the sense of a "mutual subjection" of both "out of reverence for Christ." The measure of true spousal love finds its deepest source in Christ, who is the Bridegroom of the Church, his Bride.

The symbolic dimension of the "great mystery"

25. In the Letter to the Ephesians we encounter *a second dimension* of the analogy which, taken as a whole, serves to reveal the "great mystery." This is *a symbolic dimension*. If God's love for the human person, for the Chosen People of Israel, is presented by the Prophets as the love of the bridegroom for the bride, such

an analogy expresses the "spousal" quality and the divine and non-human character of God's love: "For your Maker is your husband. . . the God of the whole earth he is called" (*Is* 54:5). The same can also be said of the spousal love of Christ the Redeemer: "For God so loved the world that he gave his only Son" (*Jn* 3:16). It is a matter, therefore, of God's love expressed by means of the Redemption accomplished by Christ. According to Saint Paul's Letter, this love is "like" the spousal love of human spouses, but naturally it is not "the same." For the analogy implies a likeness, while at the same time leaving ample room for nonlikeness.

This is easily seen in regard to the person of the "bride." According to the Letter to the Ephesians, the bride *is the Church,* just as for the Prophets the bride was Israel. She is therefore *a collective subject* and not *an individual person.* This collective subject is the People of God, a community made up of many persons, both women and men. "Christ has loved the Church" precisely as a community, as the People of God. At the same time, in this Church, which in the same passage is also called his "body" (cf. *Eph* 5:23), he has loved every individual person. For Christ has redeemed all without exception, every man and woman. It is precisely this love of God which is expressed in the Redemption; the spousal character of this love reaches completion in the history of humanity and of the world.

Christ has entered this history and remains in it as the Bridegroom who "has given himself." "To give" means "to become a sincere gift" in the most complete and radical way: "Greater love has no man than this" (*Jn* 15:13). According to this conception, *all human beings — both women and men — are called* through the Church, *to be the "Bride" of Christ, the Redeemer of the world.* In this way "being the bride," and thus the "feminine" element, becomes a symbol of all that is "human," according to the words of Paul: "There is neither male nor female; for you are all *one* in Christ Jesus" (*Gal* 3:28).

From a linguistic viewpoint we can say that the analogy of spousal love found in the Letter to the Ephesians links what is "masculine" to what is "feminine," since, as members of the Church, men too are included in the concept of "Bride." This should not surprise us, for Saint Paul, in order to express his mission in Christ and in the Church, speaks of the "little children with whom he is again in travail" (cf. *Gal* 4:19). In the sphere of what is "human" — of what is humanly personal — *"masculinity" and "femininity" are distinct,* yet at the same time they *complete and explain each other.* This is also present in the great analogy of the "Bride" in the Letter to the Ephesians. In the Church every human being — male and female — is the "Bride," in that he or she accepts the gift of the love of Christ the Redeemer, and seeks to respond to it with the gift of his or her own person.

Christ is the Bridegroom. This expresses the truth about the love of God who "first loved us" (cf. *1 Jn* 4:19) and who, with the gift generated by this spousal love for man, has exceeded all human expectations: "He loved them to the end" (*Jn* 13:1). The Bridegroom — the Son consubstantial with the Father as God — became the son of Mary; he became the "son of man," true man, a male. *The symbol of the Bridegroom is masculine.* This masculine symbol represents the human aspect of the divine love which God has for Israel, for the Church, and for all people. Meditating on what the Gospels say about Christ's attitude towards women, we can conclude that *as a man,* a son of Israel, he *revealed* the dignity of the "daughters of Abraham" (cf. *Lk* 13:16), *the dignity belonging to women* from the very "beginning" on an equal footing with men. At the same time Christ emphasized the originality which distinguishes women from men, all the richness lavished upon women in the mystery of creation. Christ's attitude towards women serves as a model of what the Letter to the Ephesians expresses with the concept of "bridegroom." Precisely because Christ's divine love is the love of a Bridegroom, it is the model and pattern of all human love, men's love in particular.

The Eucharist

26. Against the broad background of the "great mystery" expressed in the spousal relationship between Christ and the Church, it is possible to understand adequately the calling of the "Twelve." *In calling only men as his Apostles,* Christ acted *in a completely free and sovereign manner.* In doing so, he exercised the same freedom with which, in all his behavior, he emphasized the dignity and the vocation of women, without conforming to the prevailing customs and to the traditions sanctioned by the legislation of the time. Consequently, the assumption that he called men to be apostles in order to conform with the widespread mentality of his times, does not at all correspond to Christ's way of acting. "Teacher, we know that you are true, and teach the way of God truthfully, and care for no man; for *you do not regard the position of men"* (*Mt* 22:16). These words fully characterize *Jesus of Nazareth's behavior.* Here one also finds an explanation for the calling of the "Twelve." They are with Christ at the Last Supper. They alone receive the sacramental charge, "Do this in remembrance of me" (*Lk* 22:19; *1 Cor* 11:24), which is joined to the institution of the Eucharist. On Easter Sunday night they receive the Holy Spirit for the forgiveness of sins: "Whose sins you forgive are forgiven them, and whose sins you retain are retained" (*Jn* 20:23).

We find ourselves at the very heart of the Paschal Mystery, which completely reveals the spousal love of God. Christ is the Bridegroom because "he has given himself": his body has been "given," his blood has been "poured out" (cf. *Lk* 22:19-20). In this way "he loved them to the end" (*Jn* 13:1). The "sincere gift" contained in the Sacrifice of the Cross gives definitive prominence to the spousal meaning of God's love. As the Redeemer of the world, Christ is the Bridegroom of the Church. *The Eucharist is the Sacrament of our Redemption.* It is *the Sacrament of the Bridegroom and of the Bride.* The Eucharist makes present and realizes anew in a sacramental manner the redemptive act of Christ, who "creates" the Church, his body. Christ is united with this "body" as the bridegroom with the bride. All this is contained in the Letter to the Ephesians. The perennial "unity of the two" that exists between man and woman from the very "beginning" is introduced into this "great mystery" of Christ and of the Church.

Since Christ, in instituting the Eucharist, linked it in such an explicit way to the priestly service of the Apostles, it is legitimate to conclude that he thereby wished to express the relationship between man and woman, between what is "feminine" and what is "masculine." It is a relationship willed by God both in the mystery of creation and in the mystery of Redemption. It is *the Eucharist* above all that expresses *the redemptive act of Christ the Bridegroom towards the Church the Bride.* This is clear and unambiguous when the sacramental ministry of the Eucharist, in which the priest acts *"in persona Christi,"* is performed by a man. This explanation confirms the teaching of the Declaration *Inter Insigniores,* published at the behest of Paul VI in response to the question concerning the admission of women to the ministerial priesthood.[50]

The Gift of the Bride

27. The Second Vatican Council renewed the Church's awareness of the universality of the priesthood. In the New Covenant there is only one sacrifice and only one priest: Christ. *All the baptized share in the one priesthood of Christ,* both men and women, inasmuch as they must "present their bodies as a living sacrifice, holy and acceptable to God (cf. *Rom* 12:1), give witness to Christ in every place, and give an explanation to anyone who asks the reason for the hope in eternal life that is in them (cf. *1 Pt* 3:15)."[51] Universal participation in Christ's sacrifice, in which the Redeemer has offered to the Father the whole world and humanity in particular, brings it about that all in the Church are "a kingdom of priests" (*Rev* 5:10; cf. *1 Pt* 2:9), who not only share in the priestly mission but also in the prophetic and kingly mission of Christ the Messiah. Furthermore, this participation determines the organic unity of the Church, the People of God, with Christ. It expresses at the same time the "great mystery" described in the Letter to the Ephesians: *the bride united to her Bridegroom;* united, because she lives his life; united, because she shares in his threefold mission *(tria munera Christi);* united *in such a manner as to respond* with a "sincere gift"of self *to the inexpressible gift of the love of the Bridegroom,* the Redeemer of the world. This concerns everyone in the Church, women as well as men. It obviously concerns those who share in the ministerial priesthood,"[52] which is characterized by service. In the context of the "great mystery" of Christ and of the Church, all are called to respond — as a bride — with the gift of their lives to the inexpressible gift of the love of Christ, who alone, as the Redeemer of the world, is the Church's Bridegroom. The "royal priesthood," which is universal, at the same time expresses the gift of the Bride.

This is of *fundamental importance for understanding the Church in her own essence,* so as to avoid applying to the Church — even in her dimension as an "institution" made up of human beings and forming part of history — criteria of understanding and judgment which do not pertain to her nature. Although the Church possesses a "hierarchical" structure,[53] nevertheless this structure is totally ordered to the holiness of Christ's members. And holiness is measured according to the "great mystery" in which the Bride responds with the gift of love to the gift of the Bridegroom. She does this "in the Holy Spirit," since "God's love has been poured into our hearts through the Holy Spirit who has been given to us" (*Rom* 5:5). The Second Vatican Council, confirming the teaching of the whole of tradition, recalled that in the hierarchy of holiness it is *precisely the "woman,"* Mary of Nazareth, who is the "figure" of the Church. She "precedes" everyone on the path to holiness; in her person "the Church has already reached that perfection whereby she exists without spot or wrinkle (cf. *Eph* 5:27)."[54] In this sense, one can say that the Church is *both* "Marian" and "Apostolic-Petrine."[55]

In the history of the Church, even from earliest times, there were side-by-side with men *a number of women,* for whom the response of the Bride to the Bridegroom's redemptive love acquired full expressive force. First we see those women who had personally encountered Christ and followed him. After his departure, together with the Apostles, they "devoted themselves to prayer" in the Upper Room in Jerusalem until the day of Pentecost. On that day the Holy Spirit spoke through "the sons and daughters" of the People of God, thus fulfilling the words of the prophet Joel (cf. *Acts* 2:17). These women, and others afterwards, played *an active and important role in the life of the early Church,* in building up from its foundations the first Christian community — and subsequent communities — *through their own charisms and their varied service.* The apostolic writings note their names, such as Phoebe, "a deaconess of the Church at Cenchreae" (cf. *Rom* 16:1), Prisca with her husband Aquila (cf. *2 Tim* 4:19), Euodia and Syntyche (cf. *Phil* 4:2), Mary, Tryphaena, Persis, and Tryphosa (cf. *Rom* 16:6, 12). Saint Paul speaks of their "hard work" for Christ, and this hard work indicates the various fields of the Church's apostolic service, beginning with the "domestic Church." For in the latter, "sincere faith" passes from the mother to her children and grandchildren, as was the case in the house of Timothy (cf. *2 Tim* 1:5).

The same thing is repeated down the centuries, from one generation to the next, as *the history of the Church* demonstrates. By defending the dignity of women and their vocation, the Church has shown honor and gratitude for those women who — faithful to the Gospel - have shared in every age in the apostolic mission of the whole People of God. They are the holy martyrs, virgins, and mothers of families, who bravely bore witness to their faith and passed on the Church's faith and tradition by bringing up their children in the spirit of the Gospel.

In every age and in every country we find many "perfect" women (cf. *Prov.* 31:10) who, despite persecution, difficulties and discrimination, have shared in the Church's mission. It suffices to mention: Monica, the mother of Augustine, Macrina, Olga of Kiev, Matilda of Tuscany, Hedwig of Silesia, Jadwiga of Cracow, Elizabeth of Thuringia, Birgitta of Sweden, Joan of Arc, Rose of Lima, Elizabeth Ann Seton and Mary Ward.

The witness and the achievements of Christian women have had a significant impact on the life of the Church as well as of society. Even in the face of serious social discrimination, holy women have acted "freely," strengthened by their union with Christ. Such union and freedom rooted in God explain, for example, the great work of Saint Catherine of Siena in the life of the Church, and the work of Saint Teresa of Jesus in the monastic life.

In our own days too the Church is constantly enriched by the witness of the many women who fulfil their vocation to holiness. Holy women are an incarnation of the feminine ideal; they are also a model for all Christians, a model of the *"sequela Christi,"* an example of how the Bride must respond with love to the love of the Bridegroom.

QUESTIONS - Session Eight

1. John Paul II, in his theology of the body, returned to the fundamental truth about the relationship between God and His creation. Marriage is described as the "primordial sacrament," meaning that it lies at the very foundation of our being — since man, in the image and likeness of God, is made for intimate communion with God and others — thus he is completed by spousal love.

    Q. Explain "spousal love." How is it applied to God and His people?

2. **Q. What are the two dimensions of the analogy of spousal love (*MD*, 23)?**

3. **Q. If spousal love is the backdrop to creation, then what does that say about women, who are called to be icons of the Bride?**

4. **Q. What do we mean by saying Mary is a "figure" or "type"[6] of the Church?**

---

[6] "Type" and "figure" are theological terms meaning models, examples or forerunners. For example, Moses is considered a type of Christ because he led the People of God to freedom and gave the Law. Christ brings the new People of God into freedom from the bondage of sin and gives the new Law of the Covenant of love. Another example is Jonah in the whale as a type of Christ rising from the dead on the third day.

5. In this pivotal time in the history of the Church, so much attention is being paid to women and their vocation. The Holy Father concludes this chapter by saying that no one can have an "adequate hermeneutic" of humanity without "appropriate reference to what is 'feminine'" (*MD*, 22, para.3).

   Q. Why does the Pope say the feminine becomes the symbol of all humanity (25)?

6. **Q. Why does Christ call only men to be priests?**

7. **Q. How do all the baptized share in the "universal priesthood" of Christ?**

Father, Protector and Provider

The role of father is scripturally based. The Lord calls families within the body of Christ to be established and function according to His plan. In *Job* 29:7-17,21-25 we learn that the husband, as head of the household, is to be both respected and revered by his wife, their children and those in his household. This respect is due him because of his position of authority in the family given to him by God.

His relationship to his wife is as Christ to the Church. He is to provide for her, protect her and guide her. But this service is to be mutual. The Gospel innovation is that this mutual subjection must "gradually establish itself in hearts, consciences, behavior and customs." Women, as wives and daughters, are to honor him as the head of the family whose authority comes from the Lord (*Eph.* 5:21-31,33).

In Joshua 24:15 and Acts 16:31 we read that the husband is accountable before God for the spiritual welfare and direction of his family. He is to direct and lead his family and bring his wife and children to the Lord with a mature formation. A father can do this only if he is strong in his position as husband and father, for only then can he project the image of the loving Heavenly Father.

Not all women are called to the vocation of wife and mother. For those who are, it is important to realize that, although motherhood is natural because we physically nurture the child for nine months before birth and bring that child into the world, fatherhood is not natural but cultural. It is essential, therefore, that each wife encourage and support her husband in the role to which he has been called so he can be most effective. Four questions for a wife to ask herself when evaluating her support of her husband are:

1. Do I **accept** him for who he is, just as he is, not just tolerate but truly accept him? Acceptance constitutes seeing both his strengths and weaknesses. It means allowing him to be himself, not what I think he should be. It means to accept him at face value, looking at his strengths and allowing him to follow his convictions. Remember, God gives us the Grace to bear each other's faults. Turn to the Lord for strength and follow His example of unconditional love.

2. Do I truly **appreciate** him? Do I look only at the superficial aspects of appearance, money and success, or am I able to see his full worth; his character (honesty, dependability, kindness), his intelligence (education, knowledge, good judgment, creativity) and the many things he does for the family?

3. Do I tell him of my appreciation for him? Do I **admire** him, his manliness, his masculine skills and abilities, his achievements, his goals, his dreams and especially the way he provides for his family?

4. Do I **affirm** him and make him number one in my life? Does he take precedence over the children, the home, parents etc.? Do I prove this through my actions?

VIII
"The Greatest of These Is Love"

In the Face of Changes

28. "The Church believes that Christ, who died and was raised up for all, can through his Spirit offer man the light and the strength to respond to his supreme destiny."[56] We can apply these words of the Conciliar Constitution *Gaudium et Spes* to the present reflections. The particular reference to the dignity of women and their vocation, precisely in our time, can and must be received in the "light and power" which the Spirit grants to human beings, including the people of our own age, which is marked by so many different transformations. The Church "holds that in her Lord and Master can be found the key, the focal point, and the goal" of man and "of all human history," and she "maintains *that beneath all changes there are many realities which do not change and which have their ultimate foundation in Christ,* who is the same yesterday and today, yes and forever."[57]

These words of the Constitution on the Church in the Modern World show the path to be followed in undertaking the tasks connected with the dignity and vocation of women, against the background of the significant changes of our times. We can face these changes correctly and adequately only if we go back to the foundations which are to be found in Christ, to those "immutable" truths and values of which he himself remains the "faithful witness" (cf. *Rev.* 1:5) and Teacher. A different way of acting would lead to doubtful, if not actually erroneous and deceptive results.

The Dignity of Women and the Order of Love

29. The passage from the Letter to the Ephesians already quoted (5:21-33), in which the relationship between Christ and the Church is presented as the link between the Bridegroom and the Bride, also makes reference to the institution of marriage as recorded in the Book of Genesis (cf. 2:24). This passage connects the truth about marriage as a primordial sacrament with the creation of man and woman in the image and likeness of God (cf. *Gen* 1:27; 5:1). The significant comparison in the Letter to the Ephesians gives perfect clarity to *what is decisive for the dignity of women both in the eyes of God* — the Creator and Redeemer — *and in the eyes of human beings* — men and women. In God's eternal plan, woman is the one in whom the order of love in the created world of persons takes first root. The order of love belongs to the intimate life of God himself, the life of the Trinity. In the intimate life of God, the Holy Spirit is the personal hypostasis of love. Through the Spirit, Uncreated Gift, love becomes a gift for created persons. *Love, which is of God, communicates itself to creatures:* "God's love has been poured into our hearts through the Holy Spirit who has been given to us" (*Rom* 5:5).

The calling of woman into existence at man's side as "a helper fit for him" (*Gen* 2:18) in the "unity of the two," provides the visible world of creatures with particular conditions so that "the love of God may be poured into the hearts" of the beings created in his image. When the author of the Letter to the Ephesians calls Christ "the Bridegroom" and the Church "the Bride," he indirectly confirms through this analogy the truth about woman as bride. The Bridegroom is the one who loves. The Bride is loved: it is she who receives love, in order to love in return.

Rereading Genesis in light of the spousal symbol in the Letter to the Ephesians enables us to grasp a truth which seems to determine in an essential manner the question of women's dignity, and, subsequently, also the question of their vocation: the dignity of women is measured by the order of love, which is essentially the order of justice and charity.[58]

Only a person can love and only a person can be loved. This statement is primarily ontological in nature, and it gives rise to an ethical affirmation. Love is an ontological and ethical requirement of the person. The person must be loved, since love alone corresponds to what the person is. This explains *the commandment of love*, known already in the Old Testament (cf. *Deut* 6:5; *Lev* 19:18) and placed by Christ at the very center of the Gospel "ethos" (cf. *Mt* 22:36-40; *Mk* 12:28-34). This also explains t*he primacy of love* expressed by Saint Paul in the First Letter to the Corinthians: "the greatest of these is love" (cf. 13:13).

Unless we refer to this order and primacy we cannot give a complete and adequate answer to the question about women's dignity and vocation. When we say that the woman is the one who receives love in order to love in return, this refers not only or above all to the specific spousal relationship of marriage. It means something more universal, based on the very fact of her being a woman within all the interpersonal relationships which, in the most varied ways, shape society and structure the interaction between all persons — men and women. In this broad and diversified context, *a woman represents a particular value by the fact that she is a human person,* and, at the same time, this particular person, *by the fact of her femininity*. This concerns each and every woman, independently of the cultural context in which she lives, and independently of her spiritual, psychological and physical characteristics, as for example, age, education, health, work, and whether she is married or single.

The passage from the Letter to the Ephesians which we have been considering enables us to think of a special kind of "prophetism" that belongs to women in their femininity. The analogy of the Bridegroom and the Bride speaks of the love with which every human being — man and woman — is loved by God in Christ. But in the context of the biblical analogy and the text's interior logic, it is precisely the woman — the bride — who manifests this truth to everyone. This *"prophetic" character of women in their femininity* finds its highest expression in the Virgin Mother of God. She emphasizes, in the fullest and most direct way, the intimate linking of the order of love — which enters the world of human persons through a Woman — with the Holy Spirit. At the Annunciation Mary hears the words: "The Holy Spirit will come upon you" (*Lk* 1:35).

Awareness of a mission

30. A woman's dignity is closely connected with the love which she receives by the very reason of her femininity; it is likewise connected with *the love which she gives in return*. The truth about the person and

about love is thus confirmed. With regard to the truth about the person, we must turn again to the Second Vatican Council: "Man, who is the only creature on earth that God willed for its own sake, cannot fully find himself except through a sincere gift of self."[59] This applies to every human being, as a person created in God's image, whether man or woman. This ontological affirmation also indicates the ethical dimension of a person's vocation. *Woman can only find herself by giving love to others.*

From the "beginning," woman — like man — was created and "placed" by God in this order of love. The sin of the first parents did not destroy this order, nor irreversibly cancel it out. This is proved by the words of the Proto-evangelium (cf. *Gen* 3:15). Our reflections have focused on *the particular place occupied by the "woman"* in this key text of revelation. It is also to be noted how the same Woman, who attains the position of a biblical "exemplar," also appears within the eschatological perspective of the world and of humanity given in the Book of Revelation.60. She is *"a woman clothed with the sun,"* with the moon under her feet, and on her head a crown of stars (cf. *Rev* 12:1). One can say she is a Woman of cosmic scale, on a scale with the whole work of creation. At the same time she is "suffering the pangs and anguish of childbirth" (*Rev* 12:2) like Eve "the mother of all the living" (*Gen* 3:20). She also suffers because "before the woman who is about to give birth" (cf. Rev 12:4) there stands "the great dragon. . . that ancient serpent" (*Rev* 12:9), already known from the Proto-evangelium: the Evil One, the "father of lies" and of sin (cf. *Jn* 8:44). The "ancient serpent" wishes to devour "the child." While we see in this text an echo of the Infancy Narrative (cf. *Mt* 2:13,16), we can also see that the struggle with evil and the Evil One marks the biblical exemplar of the "woman" from the beginning to the end of history. It is also *a struggle for man, for his true good, for his salvation.* Is not the Bible trying to tell us that it is precisely in the "woman" — Eve-Mary — that history witnesses a dramatic struggle for every human being, the struggle for his or her fundamental "yes" or "no" to God and God's eternal plan for humanity?

While the dignity of woman witnesses to the love which she receives in order to love in return, the biblical "exemplar" of the Woman also seems to reveal *the true order of love which constitutes woman's own vocation.* Vocation is meant here in its fundamental, and one may say universal significance, a significance which is then actualized and expressed in women's many different "vocations" in the Church and the world.

The moral and spiritual strength of a woman is joined to her awareness that *God entrusts the human being to her in a special way.* Of course, God entrusts every human being to each and every other human being. But this entrusting concerns women in a special way — precisely by reason of their femininity — and this in a particular way determines their vocation.

The moral force of women, which draws strength from this awareness and this entrusting, expresses itself in a great number of figures of the Old Testament, of the time of Christ, and of later ages right up to our own day.

A woman is strong because of her awareness of this entrusting, strong

71

because of the fact that God "entrusts the human being to her," always and in every way, even in the situations of social discrimination in which she may find herself. This awareness and this fundamental vocation speak to women of the dignity which they receive from God himself, and this makes them "strong" and strengthens their vocation.

Thus the "perfect woman" (cf. *Prov* 31:10) becomes an irreplaceable support and source of spiritual strength for other people, who perceive the great energies of her spirit. These "perfect women" are owed much by their families, and sometimes by whole nations.

In our own time, the successes of science and technology make it possible to attain material well-being to a degree hitherto unknown. While this favors some, it pushes others to the edges of society. In this way, unilateral progress can also lead to a gradual *loss of sensitivity for man, that is, for what is essentially human.* In this sense, our time in particular *awaits the manifestation* of that "genius" which belongs to women, and which can ensure sensitivity for human beings in every circumstance: because they are human! — and because "the greatest of these is love" (cf. *1 Cor* 13:13).

Thus a careful reading of the biblical exemplar of the Woman — from the Book of Genesis to the Book of Revelation — confirms that which constitutes women's dignity and vocation, as well as that which is unchangeable and ever relevant in them, because it has its "ultimate foundation in Christ, who is the same yesterday and today, yes and forever."[61] If the human being is entrusted by God to women in a particular way, does not this mean that *Christ looks to them for the accomplishment of the "royal priesthood"* (*1 Pt* 2:9), which is the treasure he has given to every individual? Christ, as the supreme and only priest of the New and Eternal Covenant, and as the Bridegroom of the Church, does not cease to submit this same inheritance to the Father through the Spirit, so that God may be "everything to everyone" (*1 Cor* 15:28).[62] Then the truth that "the greatest of these is love" (cf. *1 Cor* 13:13) will have its definitive fulfillment.

QUESTIONS - Session Nine

1. Q. What does the Pope say is "decisive for the dignity of women"?

2. Q. What is the "prophetic" character of women in their femininity?

3. Q. How is the Virgin Mother of God the highest expression of this prophetic role?

4. Each woman is called to repeat the words of the Blessed Mother: "Behold the handmaid of the Lord. Let it be done to me according to your word." By now, we can understand better the ways in which the secular world struggles against femininity, motherhood, or patriarchy because of various misconceptions — imagined or deliberate.
   Q. How does Mary's role in salvation apply to women? To you in particular?

5. The Holy Father associates women with "entrustment" (*MD*, 30).
   Q. How does the Pope relate entrustment to the universal and fundamental vocation of women?

6. If a woman's primary vocation is to love, how does this become practically manifest in the various arenas in which she works, lives, and collaborates?

Humanity Entrusted To Women

Modern society is on the verge of collapse; a "culture of death" and distrust seems to be gaining strength. God has entrusted humanity to women in a special way by the most basic relationship of mother and child. For a "civilization of love" and life to conquer, Jesus is asking women to say "yes" to Him, to stand up for the Truth, to touch hearts one by one, to transform the world. Relationships in a healthy society are not based upon "rights" but upon "trust." Only women can restore the lost trust by being pro-life and pro-Church, because much of the loss of trust is due to radical feminism's emphasis on abortion and rejection of authority.

Must the ultimate defense of the Church today come from women? As part of the ministry of entrustment, exemplified by Mary and participated in by all women, the trustworthiness of the motherhood of the Church herself has been entrusted to the witness of women . . . . Perhaps, there is no more urgent task for women in the Church today than this one. For, as the Pope has pointed out, the maternal faith of Mary precedes the male witness of the apostles. What does this mean to us?

If the Pope is correct in locating 'entrustment' in the mother-child relationship, then a renewal of trust must begin there and it must be initiated by women. Not only our children, but even the men of our society and our Church, look to the women for guidance in what can and cannot be trusted. The servants at Cana sought out Mary, not because she could solve their problem, but because they trusted she would know where the solution could be found.

Today our world is looking desperately for solutions to scores of problems. In this situation, what is required, are confident women able to advise, 'Do whatever He tells you,' and to point to the Church as the place where we learn what it is He asks. Without this maternal, Marian trust and entrusting, there is no possibility at all that the truth of Christ can find a home in the hearts of humanity today.

The following quotation gives further evidence of John Paul II's great confidence in women.

> "Evidently assuming as a foundation what he has already asserted in *Redemptoris Mater* and *Mulieris Dignitatem*, the Pope simply stated in his post-synodal apostolic exhortation *Christifideles Laici* that 'two great tasks entrusted to women merit the attention of everyone': 'the task of bringing full dignity to conjugal life and to motherhood' and the task of assuring the moral dimension of culture'."

The Pope spoke a great deal on women throughout 1995 in conjunction with the UN Year of the Woman. In his Angelus message of June 18, 1995 he said that "the very future of the world depends so much on the awareness women have of themselves and on the proper recognition which should be guaranteed to them."

SESSION TEN - Article 31

Women and Jesus Christ - To the Third Millennium

IX
CONCLUSION

If you knew the gift of God

31. "If you knew the gift of God" (*Jn* 4:10), Jesus says to the Samaritan woman during one of those remarkable conversations which show his great esteem for the dignity of women and for the vocation which enables them to share in his messianic mission.

The present reflections, now at an end, have sought to recognize, within the "gift of God," what he, as Creator and Redeemer, entrusts to women, to every woman. In the Spirit of Christ, in fact, women can discover the entire meaning of their femininity and thus be disposed to making a "sincere gift of self" to others, thereby finding themselves.

During the Marian Year *the Church desires to give thanks to the Most Holy Trinity* for the "mystery of woman" and for every woman — for that which constitutes the eternal measure of her feminine dignity, for the "great works of God," which throughout human history have been accomplished in and through her. After all, was it not in and through her that the greatest event in human history — the incarnation of God himself — was accomplished?

Therefore *the Church gives thanks for each and every woman:* for mothers, for sisters, for wives; for women consecrated to God in virginity; for women dedicated to the many human beings who await the gratuitous love of another person; for women who watch over the human persons in the family, which is the fundamental sign of the human community; for women who work professionally, and who at times are burdened by a great social responsibility; for *"perfect"* women and for "weak" women — for all women as they have come forth from the heart of God in all the beauty and richness of their femininity; as they have been embraced by his eternal love; as, together with men, they are pilgrims on this earth, which is the temporal "homeland" of all people and is transformed sometimes into a "valley of tears"; as they assume, together with men, *a common responsibility for the destiny of humanity* according to daily necessities and according to that definitive destiny which the human family has in God himself, in the bosom of the ineffable Trinity.

The Church gives thanks *for all the manifestations of the feminine "genius"* which have appeared in the course of history, in the midst of all peoples and nations; she gives thanks for all the charisms which the Holy Spirit distributes to women in the history of the People of God, for all the victories which she owes to their faith, hope and charity: she gives thanks for all *the fruits of feminine holiness.*

The Church asks at the same time that these invaluable "manifestations of the Spirit" (cf. *1 Cor* 12:4ff.), which with great generosity are poured forth upon the "daughters" of the eternal Jerusalem, may be attentively recognized and appreciated so that they may return for the common good of the Church and of humanity, especially in our times. Meditating on the biblical mystery of the "woman," the Church prays that in this mystery all women may discover themselves and their "supreme vocation." May *Mary,* who "is a model of the Church in the matter of faith, charity, and perfect union with Christ,"[63] obtain for all of us *this same "grace,"* in the Year which we have dedicated to her as we approach the third millennium from the coming of Christ.

With these sentiments, I impart the Apostolic Blessing to all the faithful, and in a special way to women, my sisters in Christ.

Given in Rome, at Saint Peter's, on 15 August, the Solemnity of the Assumption of the Blessed Virgin Mary, in the year 1988, the tenth of my Pontificate.

John Paul II

QUESTIONS - Session Ten

1. In the first lesson of this study and the opening paragraph of the document, the following quote was highlighted from the closing message of the Second Vatican Council:

    "The hour is coming, in fact has come, when the vocation of women is being acknowledged in its fullness, the hour in which women acquire in the world an influence, an effect and a power never hitherto achieved. That is why, at this moment when the human race is undergoing so deep a transformation, women imbued with a spirit of the Gospel can do so much to aid humanity in not falling."[7]

    Q. What is the "feminine genius" of which the Holy Father speaks and which he believes will transform the world? (*MD*, 30)

2. **Q. The Pope calls women to use their moral and spiritual strength for the good of the human person, so that others might know love. What is the price of fidelity to this mission to love?**

3. **Q. The Holy Father makes a brief reference to "the mystery of woman" (*MD*, 31) without expanding on that term. Given the backdrop of the entire document, what do you think he had in mind?**

---

[7] *Address of Pope Paul VI to Women* (December 8, 1965).

4. The wording of this document shows respect and support for women in so many settings — those who are single, married, consecrated, religious, professionals, "perfect," "weak," well-supported, struggling, or abandoned. Overall, it stresses gratitude to women for their fidelity, their heroic action, and their courageous witness in many walks of life.

   Q. What, then, is the common thread that the Church wants to promote about authentic femininity?

5. **Q. After having reflected so long now on the essence of womanhood, what unique gifts can women bring to the world — through the workplace, the classroom, in the political arena, in civic associations — combining professionalism with their femininity?**

6. **Q. Review the attacks on authentic femininity and the ways that it is misunderstood in the world today. Focus specifically in the way that motherhood is described by the secular world.**

7. You discover your gift by giving it; or in the words of Pope John Paul II, "woman finds herself by the sincere gift of herself to the other." The Holy Father also wrote in his *1995 World Day of Peace Message*, "When women are able fully to share their gifts with their families and the whole community, the very way in which society understands and organizes itself is improved" (*Message*, 4). The Pope is counting on women of the Church to be on the "front lines" ushering in the "civilization of love" in the Third Millennium.

   Q. Having reflected on your unique gifts or talents, what more will you do to share those gifts, to help usher in that "civilization of love"?

References:

_____Paul Evdokimov, *"Sacrement de l'Amour: Le mystere conjugal a la lumiere de la tradition ortodoxe."* Paris. 1962, p. 42.

_____Joyce A. Little, *"The Significance of Mary for Women,"* Queen of Apostolate Series, Vol. III, 1989, (World Apostolate of Fatima, P.O. Box 976, Washington, NJ 07882), pp. 19, 24-25.

_____Rev. Arthur B. Calkins, *"Totus Tuus: John Paul's II's Program of Marian Consecration and Entrustment."* New Bedford, MA. Academy of the Immaculate, 1992 (P. O. Box 667, Valatie, NY 12184), pp. 231-232.

ENDNOTES - On the Dignity and Vocation Of Women

1. The Council's Message to Women (December 8, 1965); AAS 58 (1966), 13-14.

2. Cf. Second Vatican Ecumenical Council, Pastoral Constitution on the Church in the Modern World "Gaudium et Spes," 8; 9; 60.

3. Cf. Second Vatican Ecumenical Council, Decree on the Apostolate of the Laity "Apostolicam Actuositatem," 9.

4. Cf. Pius XII, Address to Italian Women (October 21, 1945): AAS 37 (1945) 284-295; Address to the World Union of Catholic Women's Organizations (April 24, 1952), AAS 44 (1952), 420-424; Address to the participants in the XIV International Meeting of the World Union of Catholic Women's Organizations (September 29,1957): AAS 49 (1957), 906-922.

5. Cf. John XXIII, Encyclical Letter "Pacem in Terris" (April 11, 1963); AAS 55 (1963), 267-268.

6. Proclamation of St. Teresa of Jesus as a "Doctor of the Universal Church" (September 27, 1970): AAS 62 (1970), 590-596; Proclamation of St. Catherine of Siena as a "Doctor of the Universal Church" (October 4, 1970): AAS 62 (1970), 673-678.

7. Cf. MS 65 (1973), 284f.

8. Paul VI, Address to participants at the National Meeting of the Centro Italiano Femminile (December 6, 1976): "Insegnamenti di Paolo VI," XIV (1976), 1017.

9. Cf. Encyclical Letter "Redemptoris Mater" (March 25, 1987), 46: AAS 79 (1987), 424f.

10. Second Vatican Ecumenical Council, Dogmatic Constitution on the Church "Lumen Gentium," 1.

11. An illustration of the anthropological and theological significance of the "beginning" can be seen in the first part of the Wednesday General Audience Addresses dedicated to the "Theology of the Body," beginning September 5, 1979: "Insegnamenti II," 2 (1979), 234-236.

12. Second Vatican Ecumenical Council, Pastoral Constitution on the Church in the Modern World "Gaudium et Spes," 22.

13. Second Vatican Ecumenical Council, Declaration on the Relation of the Church to Non-Christian Religions "Nostra Aetate," 1.

14. Ibid., 2.

15. Second Vatican Ecumenical Council, Dogmatic Constitution on Divine Revelation "Dei Verbum," 2.

16. Already according to the Fathers of the Church the first revelation of the Trinity in the New Testament took place in the Annunciation. One reads in a homily attributed to St. Gregory Thaumaturgus: "You, O Mary, are resplendent with light in the sublime spiritual kingdom! In you the Father, who is without beginning and whose power has covered you, is glorified. In you the Son, whom you bore in the flesh, is adored. In you the Holy Spirit, who has brought about in your womb the birth of the great King, is celebrated. And it is thanks to you, O Full of grace, that the holy and consubstantial Trinity has been able to be known in the world" (Hom. 2 in Annuntiat. Virg. Mariae: PG 10, 1169). Cf. also St. Andrew of Crete, In Annuntiat. B. Mariae: PG 97, 909.

17. Cf. Second Vatican Ecumenical Council, Declaration on the Relation of the Church to Non-Christian Religions "Nostra Aetate," 2.

18. The theological doctrine on the Mother of God (Theotokos), held by many Fathers of the Church, and clarified and defined at the Council of Ephesus (DS 251) and at the Council of Chalcedon (DS 301), has been stated again by the Second Vatican Council in Chapter VIII of the Dogmatic Constitution on the Church "Lumen Gentium," 52-69. Cf. Encyclical Letter "Redemptoris Mater," 4, 31-32 and the Notes 9, 78-83: loc. cit., 365, 402-404.

19. Cf. Encyclical Letter "Redemptoris Mater," 7-11 and the texts of the Fathers cited in Note 21: loc. cit., 367-373.

20. Cf. ibid., 39-41: loc. cit., 412-418.

21. Cf. Second Vatican Ecumenical Council, Dogmatic Constitution on the Church "Lumen Gentium," 36.

22. Cf. St. Irenaeus, "Adv. haer." V, 6, 1; V, 16, 2-3: 5. Ch. 153, 72-81 and 216-221; St. Gregory of Nyssa, De hom. op. 16: PG 44, 180; In Cant Cant. hom. 2: PG 44, 805-808; St. Augustine, In Ps. 4, 8: CCL 38, 17.

23. "Persona est naturae rationalis individua substantia": Manlius Severinus Boethius, Liber de persona et duabus naturis, III: PL 64, 1343; cf. St. Thomas Aquinas, "Summa Theologiae," Ia, q. 29, art. 1.

24. Among the Fathers of the Church who affirm the fundamental equality of man and woman before God cf. Origen, In Iesu nave IX, 9: PG 12, 878; Clement of Alexandria, Paed. 1, 4: S. Ch. 70, 128-131; St. Augustine, Sermo 51, II, 3: PL 38, 334-335.

25. St. Gregory of Nyssa states: "God is above all love and the fount of love. The great John says this: 'Love is of God' and 'God is love' (1 Jn 4:7-8). The Creator has impressed this character also on us. 'By this all men will know that you are my disciples, if you have love for one another' (Jn 13:35). Therefore, if this is not present, all the image becomes disfigured" (De hom op. 5: PG 44, 137).

26. Second Vatican Ecumenical Council, Pastoral Constitution on the Church in the Modern World "Gaudium et Spes," 24.

27. Cf. Num 23:19; Hos 11:9; Is 40:18; 46:5; cf. also Fourth Lateran Council (DS 806).

28. Second Vatican Ecumenical Council, Pastoral Constitution on the Church in the Modern World "Gaudium et Spes," 13.

29. "Diabolic" from the Greek "dia-ballo" = "I divide, separate, slander."

30. Cf. Origen, "In Gen. hom." 13, 4: PG 12, 234; St. Gregory of Nyssa, De virg. 12: S. Ch. 119, 404-419; De beat. VI: PG 44, 1272.

31. Cf. Second Vatican Ecumenical Council, Pastoral Constitution on the Church in the Modern World "Gaudium et Spes," 13.

32. Cf. ibid., 24.

33. It is precisely by appealing to the divine law that the Fathers of the fourth century strongly react against the discrimination still in effect with regard to women in the customs and the civil legislation of their time. Cf. St. Gregory of Nazianzus, Or. 37, 6: PG 36, 290; St. Jerome, "Ad Oceanum" ep. 77, 3: PL 22, 691; St. Ambrose, "De instit. virg." III, 16:PL 16, 309; St. Augustine, Sermo 132, 2: PL 38, 735; Sermo 392, 4: PL 39, 1711.

34. Cf. St. Irenaeus, Adv. haer. III 23, 7: S. Ch. 211, 462-465; V, 21, 1: S. Ch. 153, 260-265; St. Epiphanius, Panar. III, 2, 78: PG 42, 728-729; St. Augustine, Enarr. in Ps. 103, S. 4, 6: CCL 40, 1525.

35. Cf. St. Justin, "Dial. cum Tryph." 100: PG 6, 709712; St. Irenaeus, "Adv. haer." III, 22, 4: S. Ch. 211, 438-445; v, 19, 1: 5. Ch. 153, 248-251; St. Cyril of Jerusalem, "Catech." 12, 15: PG 33, 741; St. John Chrysostom, "In Ps." 44, 7: PG 55, 193; St. John Damascene, "Hom. 2 in dorm." B.V.M. 3: S. Ch. 80, 130-135; Hesychius, Sermo 5 in Deiparam; PG 93, 1464f.; Tertullian, "De carne Christi" 17: CCL 2, 904f.; St. Jerome, "Epist". 22, 21: PL 22, 408; St. Augustine, "Sermo" 51, 2-3: PL 38, 335; "Sermo" 232, 2: PL 38, 1108; J. H. Newman, "A Letter to the Rev. E. B. Pusey," Longmans, London 1865; M. J. Scheeben, "Handbuch der Katholischen Dogmatik," V/1 (Freiburg 1954), 243-266; v/2 (Freiburg 1954), 306-499.

36. Second Vatican Ecumenical Council, Pastoral Constitution on the Church in the Modern World "Gaudium et Spes," 22.

37. Cf. St. Ambrose, "De instit. virg." V, 33: PL 16, 313.

38. Cf. Rabanus Maurus, "De vita beatae Mariae Magdalenae," XXVII: "Salvator...ascensionis suae eam (=Mariam Magdalenam) ad apostolos instituit apostolam" (PL 112, 1474). "Facta est Apostolorum Apostola per hoc quod ei committitur ut resurrectionem dominicam discipulis annuntiet": St. Thomas Aquinas, "In Ioannem Evangelistam Expositio," c. XX, L. III 6 ("Sancti Thomae Aquinatis Comment. in Matthaeum et Ioannem Evangelistas"), Ed. Parmen. X, 629.

39. Second Vatican Ecumenical Council, Pastoral Constitution on the Church in the Modern World "Gaudium et Spes," 24.

40. Encyclical Letter "Redemptoris Mater", 18: loc. cit., 383.

41. Cf. Second Vatican Ecumenical Council, Pastoral Constitution on the Church in the Modern World "Gaudium et Spes," 24.

42. Cf. John Paul II, Wednesday General Audience Addresses, April 7 and 21, 1982: "Insegnamenti" V, 1, (1982), 1126-1131 and 1175-1179.

43. Cf. Second Vatican Ecumenical Council, Dogmatic Constitution on the Church "Lumen Gentium," 63; St. Ambrose, In Lc II, 7: S. Ch. 45, 74; De instit. virg. XIV, 87-89: PL 16, 326-327; St. Cyril of Alexandria, Hom. 4: PG 77, 996; St. Isidore of Seville, "Allegoriae" 139: PL 83, 117.

44. Second Vatican Ecumenical Council, Dogmatic Constitution on the Church "Lumen Gentium," 63.

45. Ibid., 64.

46. Ibid., 64.

47. Ibid., 64. Concerning the relation Mary-Church which continuously recurs in the reflection of the Fathers of the Church and of the entire Christian Tradition, cf. Encyclical Letter "Redemptoris Mater," 42-44 and Notes 117-127: loc. cit., 418-422. Cf. also: Clement of Alexandria, "Paed". 1, 6: S. Ch. 70, 186f.; St. Ambrose, "In Lc" II, 7: "S. Ch." 45, 74; St. Augustine, "Sermo" 192, 2: PL 38, 1012; "Sermo" 195, 2: PL 38, 1018; "Sermo" 25, 8: PL 46, 938; St. Leo the Great, "Sermo" 25, 5: PL 54, 211; "Sermo" 26, 2: PL 54, 213; St. Bede the Venerable, "In Lc" I, 2: PL 92, 330. "Both mothers — writes Isaac of Stella, disciple of St. Bernard — both virgins, both conceive through the work of the Holy Spirit...Mary...has given birth in body to her Head; the Church...gives to this Head her body. The one and the other are mothers of Christ: but neither of the two begets him entirely without the other. Properly for that reason...that which is said in general of the virgin mother Church is understood especially of the virgin mother Mary; and that which is said in a special way of the virgin mother Mary must be attributed in general to the virgin mother Church; and all that is said about one of the two can be understood without distinction of one from the other" (Sermo 51, 7-8: S. Ch. 339, 202-205).

48. Cf. for example, Hos 1:2; 2:16-18; Jer 2:2; Ezek 16:8; Is 50:1; 54:5-8.

49. Cf. Col 3:18; 1 Pt 3:1-6; Tit 2:4-5; Eph 5:22-24; 1 Cor 11:3-16; 14:33-35; 1 Tim 2:11-15.

50. Cf. Congregation for the Doctrine of the Faith, Declaration Concerning the Question of the Admission of Women to the Ministerial Priesthood "Inter Insigniores" (October 15, 1976): A, 45, 69 (1977), 98- 116.

51. Cf. Second Vatican Ecumenical Council, Dogmatic Constitution on the Church "Lumen Gentium," 10.

52. Cf. ibid., 10.

53 Cf. ibid., 18-29.

54. Ibid., 65; cf. also 63; cf. Encyclical Letter "Redemptoris Mater," 2-6; loc. cit., 362-367.

55. "This Marian profile is also — even perhaps more so — fundamental and characteristic for the Church as is the apostolic and Petrine profile to which it is profoundly united. ...The Marian dimension of the Church is antecedent to that of the Petrine, without being in any way divided from it or being less complementary. Mary Immaculate precedes all others, including obviously Peter himself and the Apostles. This is so, not only because Peter and the Apostles, being born of the human race under the burden of sin, form part of the Church which is 'holy from out of sinners,' but also because their triple function has no other purpose except to form the Church in line with the ideal of sanctity already programmed and prefigured in Mary. A contemporary theologian has rightly stated that Mary is 'Queen of the Apostles without any pretensions to apostolic powers: she has other and greater powers' (H. U. von Balthasar, "Neue Klarstellungen")." Address to the Cardinal and Prelates of the Roman Curia (December 22, 1987); "L'Osservatore Romano," December 23, 1987. 56. Cf. Second Vatican Ecumenical Council, Pastoral Constitution on the Church in the Modern World "Gaudium et Spes," 10.

57. Ibid., 10.

58. Cf. St. Augustine, "De Trinitate," L. Viii, VII, 10-X, 14: CCL 50, 284-291.

59. Second Vatican Ecumenical Council, Pastoral Constitution on the Church in the Modern World "Gaudium et Spes," 24.

60. Cf. in the Appendix to the works of St. Ambrose, "In Apoc." IV, 3-4: PL 17, 876; St. Augustine, "De symb. ad. catech. sermo" IV: PL 40, 661.

61. Second Vatican Ecumenical Council, Pastoral Constitution on the Church in the Modern World "Gaudium et Spes," 10.

62. Second Vatican Ecumenical Council, Dogmatic Constitution on the Church "Lumen Gentium," 36.

63. Cf. ibid., 63.

THE DIGNITY AND VOCATION OF WOMEN

GLOSSARY

Article   Term

1   *Apostolicam Actuositatem*
- The Latin title of the *Decree on the Apostolate of the Laity* from the Second Vatican Council.

4   **archetype**
- from the Greek meaning a supreme model, exemplar, standard, pattern, model, prototype.

6   **anthropology**
- from two Greek words meaning Man, human, and Study of. The English word means the study of humanity; the way to understand the human person.

8   **ultra-corporeal**
- Ultra means beyond, excessive, extreme; corporeal means bodily. So this word seems to refer to excessive concern with the body. The Fatherhood of God cannot be thought of in terms of the masculine body. It has to do with the spiritual qualities. God does not have a body.

anthropomorphism
- from two Greek words meaning, "man, human" and "form, shape." It means describing God with human characteristics. For example, God became angry; God hid his face.

10   **Communio personarum**
- Latin for "communion of persons."
- Context- The pope is talking about *how* marriage unites man and woman in a total sharing of goods, spiritual and material, body and soul There union is a mutual relationship of persons of equal dignity.

concupiscence
- From Latin, *concupere, to* desire intensely or strongly. There are two meanings:
  1) the passionate desire of a person inclining the sense appetite toward a sensible good or away from a sensible evil;
  2) inclination towards evil.
- Context- The Pope refers to the scriptural references 10 the concupiscence or pleasure of the eye, flesh and the pride of life. In the sense concupiscence is used in the second, negative, sense. Concupiscence is not a sin in itself but can easily and forcefully lead to sin.

11   **progenitrix**
- From Latin progenitor, beget, parent. This is the feminine form of the word, hence, it means mother.
- Context- The Pope is pointing out the importance of the Woman in the *proto-evangelium,* the first promise of a redeemer. He uses this Latin based word for mother, perhaps to connect it with *"proto-evangelium"*.

13 **mite**
   - A mite was a small coin of very little value, perhaps half a penny. Jesus told the parable of a widow who gave a mite, all she had, to the temple. Jesus praises this woman's example of generosity.

sociojuridical
   - Socio- is a prefix meaning social or society. Joined with the word "juridical" which pertains to law, it means the laws governing society, or the cultural milieu of the time.

22 **hermeneutic**
   - From a Greek word, *hermeneutikos,* meaning interpreter. It means the way one interprets or understands something, especially Scripture.
   - Context- In this sentence simply substitute the word "understanding." *...one can have no adequate understanding of man,...*

27 **charisms**
   - From a Greek word meaning divine favors, gifts, graces, spiritual powers.
   - Context- God gave women special gifts, charisms, in the service and building up of the early Church. He continues to do so today in accordance with the natural talents and qualities of women.

29 **primordial**
   - From Latin, *primordialis* first in sequence of time, original, fundamental, primary.
   - Context- the Pope writes that marriage is the primordial sacrament, that it is, the first sacrament. It was instituted at the creation of man and woman in the image and likeness of God. In a way, it is a sacrament before there were sacraments. It is the first sacrament.

Gaudium et Spes
   - This is the Latin title for the *Pastoral Constitution on the Church in the Modern World,* a document from the Second Vatican Council. Church documents receive their names from the first few words. In this case, these words mean, "The *joys and hopes...."* This is one of the more important documents issued by the Council. Pope John Paul II was one of the authors and he frequently quotes from it.

hypostasis
   - See hypostatic union in unit on Mary. From the Greek meaning the essence or substance of something. That which makes a thing to be what it is. When the essence has intelligence, the hypostasis is the personality, or quality of a person.
   - Context- The Holy Spirit is the essence of love. The Holy Spirit is Love, a personal love. Love is a Person, the Holy Spirit. "God is Love" (*1 Jn.* 4:4).

ontological
   - From the Greek, *ontos,* being, existence. Ontology is the philosophy of the nature of being.

ethos
   - The character, values, disposition of a specific person or group.
   - Context- The "Gospel ethos" includes the values, teaching manner of conduct, etc. Jesus gave us.

primacy of love
   - Primacy means, first, foremost. The phrase means love is supreme over all other values.

It is the most important reality.

prophetism
- Prophecy has to do with revealing the divine will, proclaiming God's message.
- Context- Woman's femininity has a prophetic character. Woman's very nature proclaims God's message of His loving relationship to humanity. God loves us as Bridegroom to Bride, man to woman, Christ to Christ. Woman is the supreme example of all humanity in relation to God.

interior logic
- It simply means the logic *within* the Scripture text.

30 **Proto-evangelium**
- From the Greek, *proto,* first; and *evangelium,* good news, gospel.
- Context- The term refers to the text of *Gen* 3:15 where God first promises to send a Redeemer to fallen humanity.

exemplar
- See exemplar in Redemptoris Mater unit. It means example, model.
- Context- The image of the Woman becomes an important figure, example, model in the Bible.

eschatological
- From the Greek, *eschatos,* meaning last. Concerning the last things: death, human destiny, final judgement, end/renewal of the world, coming and eternal reign of Christ, heaven and hell.
- Context- The supreme example or role model of the Woman in the Bible is not only at the beginning in Genesis, but in the Book of Revelation at the final judgment and coming of Christ.

royal priesthood
- The phrase is used in Scripture: *Ex.* 19:5-6, *1 Pt* 2:9.
- It usually refers to the priesthood of all believers as different from the ordained ministerial priesthood of clerics. It is the priesthood whereby all the faithful share in Christ's priesthood by offering a sacrifice of praise to God, offering their bodies and lives (*Rom* 12:1f). The royal priesthood of the faithful gives worship to God and strives to live in holiness.
- Context- Every person in Christ is to live a life of worship and holiness, but Christ looks to women especially to show people how to do it in their daily lives. Woman, who is primarily a person of love, best models worship and holiness, which are the human response of love toward God.

Leader's Guide

Feminine Genius
- A phrase coined by Pope John Paul II to express the many qualities, attributes, talents, inclinations, intellectual and creative powers which are woman's by nature. These include love, generosity, self-giving, patience, nurturing, sensitivity to others, etc..

THE DIGNITY AND VOCATION OF WOMEN

Please take a minute or two to give us some Feedback.

Program: _____ Male: ☐ Female: ☐

Single: ☐   Engaged: ☐   Married: ☐   Have children: ☐ (check all boxes that apply)

1. Of the TOGETHER! group meetings held this year, how many have you attended?

    ☐ All   ☐ Most (75% or more)   ☐ Many (over half)   ☐ Some (less than half)

    Comments: _____

    _____

2. Which part(s) of the group meetings do you find most rewarding?

    (Number in order of importance to you)

    ___ Relationship with Christ in the Gospel

    ___ Teaching of the Church as revealed in the documents studied

    ___ Catechesis

    Comments: _____

    _____

3. Did the group meetings help you understand your Faith and the teaching of the Catholic Church?

    ☐ Definitely   ☐ Very much   ☐ Somewhat   ☐ Not much

    Comments: _____

    _____

4. Do you review the discussion material at home after the group meetings?

    ☐ Every time   ☐ Frequently   ☐ Sometimes   ☐ Never

    Comments: _____

    _____

5. Do you read the discussion material at home in preparation for the next group meeting?

    ☐ Every time   ☐ Frequently   ☐ Sometimes   ☐ Never

    Comments: _____

    _____

6. Do you plan to participate in a TOGETHER! program next year?

    ☐ Definitely   ☐ Most likely   ☐ Perhaps   ☐ No

    Which ones: _____

7. Do you discuss the study material with anyone between meetings?

☐ My spouse   ☐ Brother or sister   ☐ Close friend   ☐ Parents

☐ Other(s) _____   ☐ Nobody

Comments: _____

_____

8. Has it given you more insight into your vocation in life?

☐ Yes   ☐ No   ☐ Somewhat

Comments: _____

_____

9. Has it improved relationships with those close to you?

☐ Yes   ☐ No   ☐ Somewhat

Comments: _____

_____

7. Who do you know that may be interested in starting a TOGETHER! group in the next year?

Name: _____ Phone: _____-_____-_____

8. The following parish may be interested in starting TOGETHER! groups:

Parish: _____ City: _____

Contact: _____ Phone: _____-_____-_____

Address: _____ City _____ Zip _____

E-mail: _____ State: ___

9. The following is optional but provides us the means to notify you of upcoming programs:

My Name: _____ My group location: _____

Address: _____

_____ _____ _____

E-mail: _____

Please send the completed evaluation to the address on the back of the book.

Note: TOGETHER! does not sell, rent, lend or give out any of its address information.

Thank you! May God richly bless you!

Paul and Libbie Sellors

CPSIA information can be obtained at www.ICGtesting.com
Printed in the USA
LVOW03s0812270714

396213LV00005B/162/P

9 781933 463100